An Englishw

Rosamond Stephen's Record of the Great War

IRISH NARRATIVES

IRISH NARRATIVES

Series edited by David Fitzpatrick

Personal narratives of past lives are essential for understanding any field of history. They provide unrivalled insight into the day-to-day consequences of political, social, economic or cultural relationships. Memoirs, diaries and personal letters, whether by public figures or obscure witnesses of historical events, will often captivate the general reader as well as engrossing the specialist. Yet the vast majority of such narratives are preserved only among the manuscripts or rarities in libraries and archives scattered over the globe. The aim of this series of brief yet scholarly editions is to make available a wide range of narratives concerning Ireland and the Irish over the last four centuries. All documents, or sets of documents, are edited and introduced by specialist scholars, who guide the reader through the world in which the text was created. The chosen texts are faithfully transcribed, the biographical and local background explored, and the documents set in historical context. This series will prove invaluable for university and school teachers, providing superb material for essays and textual analysis in class. Above all, it offers a novel opportunity for readers interested in Irish history to discover fresh and exciting sources of personal testimony.

Other titles in the series:

Forthcoming titles:

David Fitzpatrick teaches history at Trinity College, Dublin. His books include *Politics and Irish Life, 1913–1921* (1977, reissued 1998), *Oceans of Consolation: Personal Accounts of Irish Migration to Australia* (1995) and *The Two Irelands, 1912–1939* (1998).

An Englishwoman in Belfast
Rosamond Stephen's Record of the Great War

Edited by
Oonagh Walsh

CORK  UNIVERSITY PRESS

First published in 2000 by
Cork University Press
Cork
Ireland

British Library Cataloguing in Publication Data
A CIP catalogue record for this book is available from the British Library.
ISBN 1 85918 270 4

Typesetting by Red Barn Publishing, Skeagh, Skibbereen, Co. Cork
Printed in Ireland by ColourBooks, Baldoyle, Co. Dublin

Contents

Acknowledgements

'The Record' is held in the Representative Church Body Library, Dublin (MS 253). I gratefully acknowledge the Representative Church Body for permission to publish these extracts. I also wish to thank Dr Susan Hood and Dr Raymond Refaussé for their courteous assistance in the preparation of this text. I am grateful for permission to use the library's pencil drawing of Rosamond Stephen for the cover illustration. This now hangs in a recently refurbished room of the library, which has been named in her memory.

Finally, thanks to David Fitzpatrick, for his meticulous and patient guidance throughout this process.

Introduction

> I do think when the time comes to sit by the fire at Stepaside it
> would be so amusing to have tons of old letters and journals and to
> write memoirs in a locked book, for the instruction of future ages.
> I am sure I could make up something that would present a real pic-
> ture of life and manners at this queer, critical, changing crisis of Irish
> history. In 30 years things will be awfully different.[1]

Letters are by their nature public documents, yet few correspondents
can have been more conscious of the potential audience for her missives
than Rosamond Stephen. Throughout her long life, she preserved her
impressions of political and religious events in letters sent to a wide cir-
cle of friends. The recipients were asked to return them so that they
could be incorporated into what she titled 'The Record'[2], a highly personal narrative which spanned the years 1902–1940. When she retired
to Carlingford, County Louth in 1932, she gathered the letters together
to form an account of the Home Rule crisis, the First World War, and
the Anglo-Irish and Civil Wars. Her consciousness of these documents
as historical records ensured that she paid close attention to the progress
of daily events, and the letters themselves indicate how important were
narratives of this sort in the dissemination of information. Stephen's
correspondents in this narrative are her sisters Dorothea, living in India
when the war broke out, and Katharine, based in Cambridge, each of
whom depended upon Rosamond for information on Irish political
events. The extracts selected concentrate upon the First World War, in
some senses the most important period of Stephen's life. She hoped that
the war would act to bind Ireland to Britain, and eliminate the desire
for independence on the part of the Irish. To encourage this happy state
of affairs, she devoted her considerable energies to persuading young
Irishmen to enlist in the British army, and fought her own war against
the rising tide of nationalist sentiment in Ireland. In both instances she
was unsuccessful, yet her commitment to these objectives, expressed in
her letters, reveals a singular personality.

Rosamond Stephen was born in London in 1868, the ninth of ten children of Sir James Fitzjames Stephen[3] and Mary Richenda Cunningham. The family were part of the political and intellectual elite in England throughout the nineteenth and early twentieth centuries, enjoying social contact with figures such as Froude, Gladstone, Carlyle, and Thackeray. Sir James Fitzjames was a High Court judge whose father, Sir James Stephen, had been Colonial Under-Secretary between 1836 and 1847, and subsequently Regius Professor of Modern History at Cambridge.[4] Sir Leslie Stephen, James Fitzjames's brother, was editor of the *Dictionary of National Biography* and the father of Virginia Woolf. Katharine, Rosamond's younger sister, was to become Principal of Newnham College, Cambridge.[5] Although not herself formally associated with any educational movement, Rosamond firmly believed in the necessity of extending education to all. Indeed, one of the most important strands of her voluntary work in Ireland was the establishment of a lending library, to be open to all faiths and classes. She built up an impressive range of texts (numbering over 5,000 by 1931), many of them works on Irish and European history as well as church history, which were eventually to form the nucleus of the present Representative Church Body Library.

Stephen's religious upbringing was unusual. She was raised as a theist, a believer in God, but her parents had abandoned religious practice when she was born. Despite a strong family association with the Church of England — her maternal grandfather[6] was Vicar of Harrow on the Hill for almost fifty years, and her paternal great-grandfather[7] was one of the founders of the Church Missionary Society — Rosamond joined the Church of Ireland as an adult. The Stephen family had spent their summers between 1875 and 1892 at Ravensdale, County Louth, and on the somewhat slender associations between happy childhood memories and a personal conviction that the Church of Ireland was the true church, she was confirmed by Archbishop Plunket[8] in 1896, at the age of 28.

Confirmation brought a determination to enter fully into Irish church life. Her position as a new arrival made her one of its most constructive critics, and even at the risk of giving offence to long-standing members Stephen made her views known. In discussing the rejection of Arthur Kavanagh by his electorate in 1880, for example, she declared that 'He was quite wrong [to take offence] . . . he ought to have said to himself that landlords have done a power of harm in Ireland, and the Irish Church has done a power of harm in Ireland, and it is for us of this generation to expiate it. If he had looked at it that way he would have put up with the pain they gave him.'[9] Throughout her life she explained her decision to join the Church of Ireland in historical as well as religious terms. Her visits to Ireland had led her to consider the matter of relations between Roman Catholics and Protestants;[10] she became convinced that she had a mission to draw the two groups together, because the Church of Ireland was 'the representative of the church established in Ireland in the later days of the Roman Empire', and therefore had claim to be the truly national church, from which Roman Catholicism had divided:

> If we are really the Catholic Church in Ireland we must work as Catholics, not for one denomination or another, but for Ireland as a whole. Our members are all the baptised people in Ireland, and those Irish people who are not baptised are, in a special manner, our charge. It is for us to win them to the church. As Catholics no part of human life is beyond our work.[11]

Stephen's ecumenical mission came at a difficult moment for the Church of Ireland, which had undergone dramatic changes in the previous thirty years. Disestablished under the Irish Church Act of 26 July 1869, the church had been coming to terms with an altered religious and political environment in the years before Stephen's confirmation. Although the church remained financially secure,[12] the declining Anglican population, especially in rural areas, was a continual source of worry. In addition, radical changes in administrative organisation had been made following disestablishment, which formed the Representative Church Body to deal with the church's finances, and empowered the hierarchy to appoint bishops, previously the right of the government. However, there

were other, less obvious, changes which impacted upon the church and
its members. The General Convention of 1870 decreed that all church
offices should be confined to men, thereby depriving women of the right
to serve on General Vestries, or to act as Churchwardens, both of which
they had been eligible to do in the past. As the nineteenth century pro-
gressed, women increasingly protested against their formal limitations,
but with little success.[13]

It was into this environment that Rosamond Stephen entered, full of
reforming enthusiasm, in 1896. Although not preoccupied with the
role of women, Stephen was nevertheless affected by church attitudes
and expectations, and she discovered a decided lack of interest in her
highly personal mission to bridge the gulf between religions. Unde-
terred, she established in 1901 the Guild of Witness as part of the
Church of Ireland Union of Prayer. She intended the Guild to act as a
positive means of integrating Irish Christians through prayer — the
'Witness' was to manifest itself through a visible and active group,
offering links within divided communities and revitalising moribund
churches. In an attempt to persuade young Church of Ireland men to
remain in Ireland, for example, an experimental technical school was
established in County Roscommon in 1911. It was hoped that the
youths would learn a trade which they would employ in Ireland, thus
maintaining church numbers in rural areas. This particular venture
ended unsuccessfully, because of limited funds and limited numbers.
Nevertheless it indicates the Guild's, and Stephen's, determination to
emphasise the church's all-Ireland nature. The Guild also established a
Sunday School for impoverished children in Belfast, which was eventually taken over by St Matthew's Church. The Guild of Witness became
in 1918 the Irish Guild of Witness, although its ecumenical purpose
remained the same. It aimed 'to promote everything that tends to witness to and develop the national and Irish character of the Church as
founded upon the labours of St. Patrick and his followers, and . . . to
strive for concord and good understanding in Ireland.'[14]

This highly individual mission brought Stephen first to Belfast,
where religious tensions ran consistently high. From 1902 to 1907,[15]

she was attached to the mission house of St. Matthew's Parish in Shankill, a Protestant and staunchly loyalist part of the city. Although charitable work was an accepted part of the lives of middle-class women in this period, Stephen's early association with evangelical mission workers caused her a great deal of difficulty in making Catholic contacts, and as the letters indicate, she was regarded with suspicion by Catholics who presumed she sought to convert them. This encounter, in 1911, demonstrates both the presumptions on the part of Catholics towards Protestant mission workers, and Stephen's own rather optimistic certainty in the success of her mission:

I am starting a little sort of lending library in place of the flower mission. So far I have five or six Roman Catholic books lent to people who were very much pleased to get them. I offered one to old Mrs. Carberry, and she said she could not read. I was just leaving when a voice growled out from behind the door 'We are not of that religion'. I saw a woman's boots under the crack of the door, so I called out round it, for it was half shut, and I in the street 'Of what religion are you then?' The owner of the boots said in a very sulky voice 'We are Roman Catholics'. 'Oh well' said I 'look here' and I pushed in and showed her I was offering the Meditations of Brother Lawrence, published by the Catholic Truth Society. She fell to and began to abuse me, I cannot remember it all, but she said in phrases drawn out by judicious questions from me that I had no business to give any but Protestant books, and that 'we were not allowed to read any but our own books, that I came giving out flowers for the Protestants, that she was the same to everyone, and did not say one thing to me and another behind my back, that many took my flowers and then said "To hell with the old . . ." that the clergy told them not to be wanting any of the flowers. Why did I come to Catholic houses? I should go to the houses of people who had no religion. "We" went regularly to Mass, and heard all we wanted to hear, and if we wanted any more we could ask our priests next door. . .' . . . It was a queer little encounter and it cheered me. Sometimes when I just trot in and out of the Roman cottages for hours, I do wonder if there is any good at all in it, and I was beginning to wonder about these books was there any real good in them. But this wild bigot, who really looked a very nice woman, made me feel that the thing is all right. I felt she and I were champions, I of something coming, she of a losing cause, and of a cause which deserves to lose because it is dead.[16]

In addition to her ecumenical quest, Stephen also sought to unite Protestants and Catholics through a re-evaluation of their shared history. In Belfast, where history had been more commonly used as a means of maintaining divisions, this was a novel and not particularly welcome innovation. Stephen had made her own contribution to historiography in the form of a children's history of Ireland, entitled *Old Days and New: A Penny History of Ireland*. Unlike the majority of historians, Stephen acknowledged her ulterior motives in writing the text:

Mr. Richard Bagwell, the historian, thought so far well of it that he tried to get it accepted as a recommended school book by the national board of education, which in those days managed the National Schools. In this he failed, but in various ways a good many copies were sold. The defect of the booklet was that I was more anxious to encourage 'united Ireland' than to study or to teach Irish history. But, as the idea of giving any historical teaching in National Schools was only then beginning to be considered, I think my booklet may have had its use in the world, though I daresay now it would be counted as beneath criticism.[17]

Throughout the war years, as a new world history was being made, Rosamond Stephen attempted to forge another historical narrative of political and religious unity. However, this unity was dependent upon Catholic nationalists accepting their position as wholly integrated members of the British Empire, something which most stubbornly refused to do. Stephen's confirmation in the Church of Ireland made her feel that she was Irish, and as the war advanced she frequently described herself as such. By 1918, she could declare 'I have lived in Ireland all my life', when in fact she had spent summer holidays there as a young woman, and did not settle full-time in the country until she was forty-four years of age.[18] While there is no doubting her good will towards Ireland, her letters suggest that she was oblivious to many of the subtleties of local politics, while time and again she displayed a striking ignorance with regard to contemporary developments. Her responses to events such as gun-running, anti-war protests, the 1916 Rising, and the conscription debate are very much those of a distanced, if opinionated, observer. Stephen was, and remained throughout the war, a liberal unionist Englishwoman, whose confidence in the efficacy of a firm hand towards the childish Irish of both denominations never wavered. Thus in February 1915 she wrote that she 'cannot conceive why people have been so slow' about recruiting, ignoring significant anti-war feeling throughout the country. Similarly, she advocated the introduction of compulsion throughout 1916 to subdue the country, without considering the likelihood of riot and rebellion. Stephen could not believe that the whole of the country did not feel as she did, and her identification with Ireland strengthened her certainty that Irish nationalism was without foundation. If she, as a self-declared Irishwoman, felt that ties to Britain should be strengthened, then the whole of the country must feel the same way, and the people with whom she came in contact in Belfast did little to alter her perceptions. Her visits to 'the cottages' (located for the most part between the Falls and Shankill roads), for example, were almost exclusively to families of enlisted men. Their natural support for the war, and enthusiasm for British victory, was interpreted as representative of the whole country, enabling Stephen to dismiss nationalist activity in Dublin as 'a minute handful of screaming Sinn Feiners'.[19] Thus although Stephen declared that her mission lay equally with Protestants as well as Catholics, she devoted far more time to the latter. This reflects the true nature of her work, which she was able to take for granted in Protestant areas, they being predominantly loyal. In fact, she found the welcome extended in Protestant areas something of a bind: 'It is very hard here not to get drawn in amongst the Protestants. All day long and every day they come to you for something, and all day long and every day the RCs push you off. It really is hard to get it fair and even.'[20]

Stephen was not however alone in many of her ambitions for Ireland, and her world view was bolstered by one important institution — the *Irish Times*. This unionist newspaper was her almost exclusive source of information for events in Dublin and beyond, but it provided more than mere facts about changing circumstances. Her letters make continual reference to reports in the newspaper which support her own political views, and she took great comfort from the fact that the newspaper refused to dignify moments of especial importance for nationalists. In her comments upon the funeral of Jeremiah O'Donovan Rossa, for example, she wrote that 'the *Irish Times* in a very obscure corner and in nearly unreadable print referred to same', and despite the large crowds in attendance ('it was estimated that about 7,000 young men were present who should have been in the army, or who were of military age, and seemed in good health') she was able to dismiss the event as of little importance: '. . . I am not sure that beyond hurting one's feelings it matters so very much.'[21] The lack of attention paid by the *Irish Times* reporter to the funeral suggests to Stephen that it represented no threat to her vision of Irish unity, despite the fact that it acted as a rallying cry for Irish nationalism.

Indeed, the very format of the *Irish Times* was a reassurance to her, and she was more anxious about missing an edition of the paper than missing letters from her sisters or mother. The suspension of publication during the 1916 Rising was a cause of great distress, but its reappearance, even in a greatly modified form, was a signal that normality had been restored to Ireland:

> On three days the paper could not be published, because all light was forbidden even a candle, and finally the boy put a copy of the dear creature in my hand, and I could have cried with pleasure to see its dirty face again. It was as the face of a friend, and a touch of common day in this nightmare. Alas dear I.T. It is a single sheet now, all its supply of paper having been used in the barricade, but news from Dublin is as I say the end of a nightmare.[22]

The paper was thus a source of reassurance as well as inspiration throughout the war, although by April 1918 she was disappointed that the realisation that its staunch line on conscription and opposition to Irish nationalism was wavering:

> And another horrid thing. The *Irish Times* is ceasing to write quite such staunch articles as it did. It is becoming silent about Ireland. It was publicly burnt at a meeting, in Navan I think it was, for the support it gave to conscription and I do not know if that affected it at all, but it writes now all about other things, there has not been an Irish article for some days. But what can it do? To speak truly about Ireland is to curse the 'King'. It is really dangerous in that way to say what you think. I am not sure that silence is not best. Loyal subjects betrayed by their King, and too sensible to become rebels are in a most awkward predicament. [23]

It was this development, rather more than the pressing evidence all around her in Belfast, which convinced Stephen that nationalism was in the ascendant. And although the *Irish Times* in fact maintained a firm line against partition, continued to support the British war effort, and celebrated the British victory in 1918, Stephen felt that vital standards had been allowed to slip.

A constant theme in these letters is that of conscription, which Stephen fervently hoped would be imposed on Ireland. Her letters record her bitter disappointment at the exclusion of Ireland from the Military Service Acts, and her certainty that conscription would be welcomed throughout the country. She pointed to the high levels of enlistment amongst Belfast Catholics as proof that that constituency was willing to sign up, but this fact tended to blind her to the growing anti-war feeling amongst most nationalists. [24] Believing that all that was required to resolve Irish opposition was a firm hand, she dismissed the increasing difficulties facing John Redmond, who was attempting to keep Home Rule hopes alive through Irish Parliamentary Party support for the war while at the same time countering the growing strength of Sinn Fein and anti-war opinion in Ireland. Ironically, Redmond believed, like Stephen, that enlistment by Catholics and Protestants would eliminate bigotry, and allow for a peaceful settlement back home.[25] She also believed that the close proximity of Catholic and Protestant men in the ranks would break down long-held prejudice, and that it would be impossible for sectarianism to survive the bonding process of service. However, although soldiers were indeed 'made one in a worthy cause', this lasted only for the duration of the war, and their return to an entirely altered political landscape shattered any prospects of building upon the experience.

What was remarkable about Stephen's views on conscription was her inability to accept that the refusal of so many young Irishmen to enlist was based upon sincerely held political beliefs. Instead, she blamed the British government for not giving them a forceful lead by implementing conscription, John Redmond for weakness of leadership, and Edward Carson for attempting to exclude any but unionists from declarations of loyalty. She was especially insensitive to Redmond's difficulties. From 1915, he had to face concerted opposition to Home Rule from within the government, as well as from nationalists in Ireland. In May, the Liberal Government had merged with the Unionist opposition, and Edward Carson, Andrew Bonar Law and A. J. Balfour became cabinet members. Their determined opposition to Home Rule made it highly unlikely that the government would be prepared to offer an acceptable settlement to Irish nationalists. Under attack at home and in London, Redmond faced an uphill political struggle, but received little sympathy or understanding from Stephen.

These letters illuminate the often contradictory attitudes towards the war which existed in Ireland. While there was large-scale recruitment amongst southern Irishmen, it was not necessarily for the reasons which Stephen had hoped. On the outbreak of war, when Redmond initially offered the Volunteers as a Home Guard, and subsequently committed them to the army, he did so as a means of ensuring that Home Rule would be granted.[26] Thus Ireland was to fight in order to secure a measure of governmental autonomy, not to strengthen the association between the two states, as Stephen desired. Similarly,

Carson's willingness to place the Ulster Volunteer Force at the army's disposal was conditional on the exclusion of Ulster from any Home Rule settlement. Neither group responded with an unambiguous declaration of loyalty — they were prepared to offer support, but for their own specific reasons. Nevertheless, the scale of Irish enlistment north and south across the four years was impressive, totalling around 206,000 men.[27] Deaths and injuries amongst the men who enlisted from 'the cottages' were common, yet in her anxiety to increase the numbers of enlisted men, Stephen gave them surprisingly little consideration. It is not that she was unsympathetic; on the contrary she was greatly distressed by deaths and injuries amongst the men of the families she visited, yet her primary goal overshadowed the very real contribution being made by Irish soldiers throughout the war. Her comments at these moments of crisis indicate the extent to which her mission rendered her extremely insensitive to others, despite a genuine concern for their welfare. She was impatient with the reservations expressed by wives and mothers over sending their men to war, describing one young woman (whose husband was later killed in action) as a 'silly giddy little wife'.[28] Similarly, she found the distress of a mother whose son was missing in action rather bemusing, declaring: 'Poor Mrs. — is nearly mad over Johnny being dead, and he was a horrid boy if ever there was one.'[29] Stephen worked steadily to assist the families of enlisted men, and used her contacts and influence to secure employment for invalided soldiers, but the urgency she experienced to increase enlistment, regardless of the price to individuals, strikes a discordant note in her letters.

At the outbreak of war, Stephen threw herself into the task of rallying support. She organised lantern-slide shows which explained British progress, and encouraged a sense of patriotism. By early 1916, however, she was increasingly critical of government policy on Irish recruitment and convinced that through its unwillingness to enforce conscription, it was frustrating Irish desire to enlist.[30] In a letter written on St. Patrick's Day in 1916, Stephen described her anger at what she regarded as the casual attitude of government towards men who

were, according to herself, more than willing to enlist if they felt they
were needed:

> Redmond and Devlin and Sinn Fein may gabble away about exclu-
> sion, but really what the poor people feel is that if the Government
> wants them it will 'fetch' them, and if it does not want them why
> they need not bother. I said to a fine youth who came here with the
> bread the other day, 'Why are you not in the Army?' and he said
> 'When the Govt. fetches me I will go with a heart and a half. But
> why should I go and leave my wife and unmarried loafers hanging
> around every corner?' I said 'Would you go if you were sure com-
> pulsion was coming?' and he said 'I would go tomorrow.' The Govt.
> is treating that man cruelly. [31]

At times, Stephen's lack of understanding of Irish nationalism led
her into endearing fantasies. After the 1916 Rising, in the course of a
conversation over the possible sentences to be given to young rebels
('boys of fifteen and sixteen'), she made the following proposal:

> 'Well if I were in charge of them, I should do like this. I should have
> each one separately out of his cell, and I should say, "Now listen to
> me. You are a very silly, naughty boy, and have been mixed up in bad
> mischief. If the King chose he might shoot you as a rebel. But you
> have a good King who does not want to shoot silly boys, but to see
> them grow into wise men. Now take your choice: will you go to
> prison for a long time, or will you take the oath of allegiance and join
> the Army? You won't get leave to go home to Ireland while the war
> lasts, but if you do well after the peace you will get a free pardon.
> And perhaps if you get the V.C. or even the D.S.O. you might get a
> pardon before the peace." ' — 'And they would all go' said Cassie,
> 'they would all become good soldiers. Cannot you get it done?' [32]

The confidence felt by Stephen in her work provoked an often con-
descending attitude towards those she visited. In particular, she patron-
ised dreadfully those who expressed any support for nationalism. Of
course, this was partly a defensive reaction on her part: if she acknowl-

edged any validity in the nationalist stance, it undermined her belief that closer union between Ireland and Britain was both possible, and desired by the people. Thus she fell back on long-standing stereotypes of Irish childishness to persuade her correspondents, but more importantly herself, that Irish political independence was the wish of the minority:

> Their whole position as Carsonites does of course rest on the Nationalists being real rebels. If the Nationalists are just silly, uneducated, tiresome people, who in the main are quite well disposed to the King, and the Empire, and only want to be a bit watched and helped in order to do reasonably well, then the whole UVF affair falls to the ground. The Nationalists who enlist and are really keen on doing their bit, for their King and Country, give the lie direct to Sir Edward.[33]

Stephen was however honest in her appraisal of politicians of all hues. Her determination to secure her objective — large-scale enlistment by Irishmen — made her view all those who appeared less than committed in the harshest possible light. She detested bluster and sham in politics, and was especially scathing of unionist leaders such as Carson. Pearse, Redmond and other nationalists may have provoked her worst tendency to patronise, but Carson was despised for his self-aggrandising postures, and his irresponsibility, as Stephen saw it, in nurturing an atmosphere of rebellion and intrigue which ultimately culminated in the 1916 Rising. When he was appointed First Lord of the Admiralty in December, 1916, she was unbridled in her criticism:

> Oh how I hate that man going to the admiralty over to the showy job in London, and leaving the people he has upset to scramble as they can out of the mess he organized. Having taken such serious steps as getting the arms and teaching the people to gabble about civil war, he ought to have stayed here and taken charge himself till the country really settles. No one could render the Empire a greater service than to help solidly in the settlement of Ireland. There must be other men for the admiralty.[34]

More deplorable still in Stephen's eyes was Carson's attempt to equate unionism solely with loyalty to the crown and country. Carson's polarisation of nationalism and unionism was, she believed, the most destructive element in Irish politics, and she did not hesitate to denounce him. Indeed, her honesty with regard to what she saw as political posturing made every public figure a potential target. Even the King came in for his share of condemnation; her statement on April 12, 1918 that the King is a coward ('How can people want to be conscripted for a cowardly King? A million times easier to conscript for a cruel tyrant') is an unexpected outburst from one who has been consistently loyal. Yet it is characteristic of Stephen. Distressed beyond measure at what she saw as the weakness of government and monarch, she apportioned blame where she believed it was due. She remained loyal not to individuals, but to an idealised vision of Britishness, which matched an equally idealised, and equally unrealistic, vision of Irishness. In 1917, she wished that Ireland could be held by force for the King, not King George, but 'for "The King", that ideal personage who ought to be enforcing righteous laws. Such a person exists ideally though not actually.'[35]

By the war's end, Stephen's mission was incomplete. Despite her best efforts, no lasting reconciliation between Catholics and Protestants had taken place, and indeed the next few years were to sunder relations between these two, as well as between Ireland and Britain, to an unimaginable extent. For most people in her position, the disappointment would have been enough to justify a return to England, and an abandonment of the work of the previous twenty years. However, it was characteristic of Stephen that she remained in Ireland, and continued to labour for the church. Between 1918 and 1928, in her capacity as Secretary and Librarian of the Irish Guild of Witness, she expanded the library holdings and encouraged its use by Guild members. When the library was presented to the Representative Church Body in 1931, to be available to all Church of Ireland members, Stephen continued to support it through generous financial donations, as well as gifts of books. She also remained active outside the church, and 'The Record' contains her vivid impressions of a changing Ireland in the years between the Anglo-Irish War and the outbreak of World War Two. After living in Dublin and Dundalk for over thirty years, Stephen finally returned to England in September 1950, to live with her sister. Her final letter to the RCB Library, written in the month before her death in February 1951, indicates her abiding interest in Irish affairs: 'Great opportunities lie now before the Church of Ireland, and much will be asked of the rising generations. The dangers look very great, but that is always the way in days of great opportunity.'[36] Forty-nine years of active church work had not quelled Rosamond Stephen's enthusiasm. Her enduring legacy to Ireland is the library which she helped to establish, but it is through 'The Record' that this solitary voice most clearly speaks.

Editorial Note

'The Record' is a typescript composed of extracts from Stephen's personal correspondence. She wished it to stand as a political and historical narrative, and therefore edited the letters herself, removing for the most part references to family matters, and retaining material which reported on current affairs. A good deal of this editorial work took place in 1947, and 'The Record' is punctuated with notes commenting upon her opinions in the earlier years. There are several gaps in the letter sequence, however, in particular between April and September 1918. There is also a good deal of repetition of news, as Stephen recounted details of the same event or incident to each sister in somewhat different ways. I have therefore selected those letters which provide a developing narrative of Stephen's experience of war, and her response to events such as the 1916 Rising and the conscription crisis. The letters have been reproduced in most cases in full, as they appear in 'The Record'.

The portion of 'The Record' which deals with the First World War consists of approximately 40,000 words, which I have reduced by one-third. Some repetitive or redundant material has been removed, and this is indicated by the summary, with an indication of the number of lost words, within square brackets. I have corrected spelling and punctuation where they distract the reader without adding to the sense of the letters, but my interventions are minor.

Rosamond Stephen

'The Record'

MS. 253, The Representative Church Body Library, Dublin.

I am frightfully upset about the recruiting. It goes on like wild fire in the UVF. All over the South it's a failure. I am sending the paper about it. For so far I can see no way out. How in the face of this am I ever to get the Protestants to believe that the others are friends, and equals. Personally it is as bad to me as a defeat. Of course I am still not at all in sympathy with Sir Edward,[1] but he is a sort of friend compared with Redmond.[2] Oh the exultation and delight in the face of an old boy I saw this morning — an upper clerk at the Bank. 'The English were all in hysterics over John Redmond' — and something in my face stopped him. He only looked. '— they have found him out now.' And all the time the Romans are absolutely loyal. I know that but how can I ask any second person to believe it. If the Bill passes or if it does not it's all the same now. In any case they are waiting to see what is going to happen instead of volunteering right off, as is their duty. The decent Home Rulers are utterly helpless. I am feeling as if I had spent all my substance for twenty years bringing up my son and as if he were now taking to drink. Perhaps in time I may think of something to be done. The general helplessness is one element in the black situation.

RS to DJS, 17 November 1914

[General remarks on recruiting, c. 450 words.] I cannot help thinking that a lot of people are just not enlisting because no one has suggested it, and that by little and little as people do suggest it they will come along. At the same time it must be allowed that in Dublin there is a certain amount of real treason. A most hateful meeting was held in Stephen's Green on Sunday urging the Irish regiments to mutiny, and saying that anybody was a slave who enlisted and so forth.[3] The government took no notice. And in T.C.D. the Gaelic Society has been forbidden to hold a meeting it was getting up because a man was to address it who took a very conspicuous anti-enlisting line.[4] I think Sinn Fein[5] is just mad at seeing how flat its anti-enlisting campaign has fallen, and people do say that German money is being very freely laid out in Dublin. Miss Finny said in her letter she knew it for certain.[6] So I personally have no opinion about that.

RS to KS, 23 November 1914

I was in the cottages this morning. Thursday made a real difference I can see that.[7] I am thankful to say they tell me that another set will go this week. They say they are trying to make up another 600. That will be awfully nice if they do. I saw one silly giddy little wife whose husband went on Thursday. Poor little thing she was almost crying, and I told her the women were very often the real heroes, because they had all the hard part and none of the fun. The Fermoy men will get passes and come home for Christmas.[8] I do hope they will take a lot back with them. No news yet of National Volunteers coming forward bodily elsewhere.

It was nice in the Roman cottages this morning. They were all so zealous, so fully in with the others. One woman said 'But our side is doing well now' and I said 'Yes. The chief thing is now to hope for a victory in Russia' and she said very anxiously, 'And which side is that?' so I said 'Oh our side of course. Russia is one of the allies', and she said with a sort of sigh of relief 'Oh that is all right. I do not know these now.' Her husband is dead and her son at the front, and her other son drinking heavily so she is not as much in society as she was.

RS to DJS, [?] 2 December 1914

Emily Wynne says the recruiting has been very bad about them.[9] The people were wild to go to the war for the first week, then they were systematically discouraged, and their zeal cooled, but a few enlist, and more now than at first. The National Volunteers about Glendalough are a very low lot, the farmers' sons will not join it. They, the N.V., are flooded with these hateful newspapers *Sinn Fein, Irish Freedom* and *Irish Labour* also with most abominable tracts from America. She saw one of them. It was printed in America, and was all about not enlisting under a foreign power, and so forth. I said Sinn Fein was oddly childish, and she agreed it appeared to be all people just emerging from the quite uneducated state. I asked what were the decent Home Rule papers, and she said *The Freeman's Journal*, the *Irish Independent*, and local rags which 'support the war as long as England does the fighting.' So I said 'How would it be if I wrote some decent articles for the decent papers,' and she quite cheered up, and said 'It would be ever such a good plan.' So I said 'I must hear of local people who would follow up my writings with the living voice, and a personal appeal, to enlist, and when I had them I would write tracts for the corner boys and nice articles for the farmers' sons.' She got quite cheered up over it.

RS to KS, 18 January 1915

Yes I got home alive from Co. Galway but it was frightfully harrowing out west. There is a strong Sinn Fein feeling and hardly any enlisting in West Connaught, except in parts of Galway, where Sinn Fein has been defeated. In Leenane a whole lot of boys fled to America to avoid conscription, and being forced to fight 'in England's army'.[10] They say 'What has England ever done for us?' and they are living on money from the Congested Districts Board, treasury grants you know from London.[11] They are of course the most ignorant of the people, led by a few hot heads. The better class of Nationalists are quite sound in theory, but do not enlist. The mitigating circumstance about that is that Galway city has not done so badly, and ever so many Claddagh[12] fishermen are in the Navy. Isn't that nice? Irish speaking sailors.

RS to KS, 22 January 1915

No, the journey did not send my temperature up. I trust that phase is past. As for the Purple Princess she has survived storms, and mountain passes, and whirling blasts, and creeping car ponies, in a manner of which I can only say it is worthy of Mrs. Carr.[13]

Recruiting seems a little better now over here. I told some of the Nationalists about the Sinn Feiners in Leenane, and they were perfectly furious, and said only a handful of people could listen to such rubbish, 'stuffing young fellows' heads with nonsense like that', 'there is no reason in it,' 'but it is only a handful,' and so on. It appears that Mayo is worse than Galway. Stephen Gwynn MP[14] member for East Galway, says that out of a total population of 15,000 for the county 1,000 men are in the Navy, and Army. As I suppose half the 15,000 are women, I should think that is a good proposition [proportion?]. Also the Claddagh has really done very well, according to the same authority 120 houses having sent 160 men into the navy.

Some of the recruits here suffer very badly from homesickness. The Protestants get it worst, poor dears, because of this idiotic plan of having the camps too near Belfast. The men at Fermoy had one frightened go of being strangers in a strange land, and then got all right, and as they had only one leave home they only had one relapse, but the Protestants come home constantly for Sunday, and, especially the married men, suffer terribly going back again, and some stay too long, and come home again without leave, and then there is ever such a row. And there is such an awful thing. I know a deserter. He left a camp in Donegal[15] without leave, and has been at home one month. I cannot imagine why the police are not after him. It is their business to catch him, and his mother is in an awful way about it. She says he is such a nuisance hanging about doing nothing, and eating like a wolf, and yet she cannot make up her mind to denounce him to anybody. The punishment for deserting in time of war is very severe, and the longer he stays the worse it gets. She has awful stories of being tried for your life, and being kept on bread and water, and being made run twice as fast as you can run round a prison yard, and your health broken for years with all you go through, and my hair stands on end to hear her, and all the more because she caretakes at our mission hall. I was round and amongst the R.C.s on Saturday. They grow more and more patriotic. One woman said 'The Kaiser thought Ireland would not stand by England. But Ireland will always stand by England, and England will always stand by Ireland.' Another said 'Really nothing else matters if England wins, but England is sure to win.'

RS to KS, 5 February 1915

Recruiting meetings are at last being held here and there in this wretched island. I cannot conceive why people have been so slow about them. They had one in Navan (Co. Meath) and 83 recruits were the result. Also Kerry is said to have now 2,000 men in the Army. I suppose that includes the reserve men. Still it seems rather a lot.

RS to KS, 12 February 1915

Two hundred recruits went from here this morning to Fermoy. They are all R.C.s who go from Clifton Street office. I saw them at the Station. One poor boy's heart failed him at the last moment, and he dashed into a public house to hide. I felt very sorry for him, especially when two vast policemen dashed in after him, and he had to walk between them into the Station (the great northern you know). However I expect he was all right once he was in the train. About young Mitchell things get worse and worse. He is ill now, and afraid to send for the doctor, lest it is found out that he has deserted. I wonder would his mother like me to denounce him to the police. Somehow I do not feel called to.

RS to DJS, 10 March 1915

I met my military church going friend again and she met some officers from the front, and they told her that the Germans are getting utterly worn out, and will collapse about July. Do you know it is so dreadful I do not wish for the end of war yet. I speak now about Belfast which I see, but I think my remarks apply also to England, from things I have picked up, in speeches and so on. I think if we win too soon, or too easily, it will go to our heads, as the victories of '71 went to the Germans' heads, and we shall be that tete montee there will be no bearing us. I very much want the UVF and the INVs to go to the front. If they do not they will grow so fearfully swaggering, and probably fall upon one another. Of course they will likely go to the front in a month or so, but if the war lasts two years it will leave us as much exhausted as Germany, and that is what I want. Here locally, a year of war would not be long enough to make Home Rule be forgotten, two years would make a much more solid barrier between then and now, and I feel after two years all the nations, and all the wise people in Europe would be crying aloud for peace, and really thankful to get it. Lloyd George said that in Paris you can see the war in everyone's face and in London people go on as if there were no war. Well so they do here in a way. I think the war at the end of the second year would be a kind of nightmare, and peace would not leave us so crowing, or so anxious to fight one another. You see we are now into the Narrows of the Dardanelles, and if and when we take Constantinople does it go to Russia? And shall we fall to fighting over it if peace comes too soon? I feel the nations will fall on one another, and on themselves, unless the war really does last a good while. It seems awful to say it, but that is how I feel.

RS to DJS, 23 March 1915

I went round some R.C. cottages to-day. The visiting is more harrowing week by week. First I went to Mrs. Mickleman and I said how was her nephew. He is like her eldest son, she brought him up. 'Oh he was home five weeks. His lungs was that bad, straight home from Indy, and into the trenches, up to his knees in water and muck. But we had him well nursed, and mended, and he was back at the front, but he took ill again, and is in hospital in Dublin.' 'And that boy?' said I, indicating a photograph of the youth who wants to be her son-in-law, 'Oh he is at the front. Has been this long time. He is alright. He writes very cheerfully. No this one (a younger boy, her own son) enlisted in the navy. He left his job and enlisted, and now I will not sign the paper giving him leave, so he cannot go and his job is lost. He is walking about, and I am feeding him.' 'But why not let him go?' 'Oh one from the house is enough. He is only 15. They would not let him go to sea yet. Yes I know it is a good life, and he would get well taken care of. I might let him go yet, I shall see.' Then I crossed to the Conways, and who should open the door but John. He was in his shirt sleeves, but I remarked that his trousers are of khaki, and a khaki coat hung over the door. He told me he had a pass to come home, because his mother was ill, and he had been up with her all night. He was rather tired, and a little low, but substantially very happy. I gave him a little French and English phrase book, and he was frightfully pleased, and really he made some not bad shots at reading the phonetically spelt words. I said if he learnt to pronounce them anyhow he would get the right pronunciation in France. He says they will leave Fermoy soon, but they are told nothing about when, and that is quite right. There are about 6,000 men there now, all recruits and the Southern recruits are coming in better now. The camp is getting known, and the men are happy there, and bring in their friends. He is a pretty fair shot now, and he can throw noiseless bombs. He will be glad to go, Fermoy is a rough place, but it is making its fortune by the troops. Well goodbye. 'Oh I hope I will see you again' and it would not have taken very much to have started him crying, he was worried about his mother, and seeing the children made him homesick. I said 'I like to read of all these distinctions in the papers. When I see about Victoria crosses and so on I say to myself "And that might happen to any of the Belfast men"' and he cheered up somewhat, and told me how 'Faugh a balla' was the motto of the Irish Fusiliers, and I said well I understood it was the Connaught Rangers turned the scale at Waterloo, being the 88th and you should have seen his face. 'Yes we did that'. Isn't it all strange beyond words? It is so very very good for a little clever talking of a man to be so pleased with what 'We' did at Waterloo. It teaches humility for one thing. From there to Rooneys. Pat is working, and Tommy is in the infirmary. You know I think both those boys are consumptive and the poor old mother has chronic bronchitis. Well I thought we were free of the war for a few minutes, but it seems that Tommy is in the ward with the frost-bitten men from the front. It was nearly impossible to get him in anywhere. The Mater[16] is full with wounded soldiers, and so is the Victoria,[17] and here the Nurse is so nice, she has promised to get him and two or three more civilian boys together at one end of the ward. The men from the front do forget themselves at times, and they do swear now and then, and at the front they get so very angry, and then they got the habit of it, but Tommy is coming over by the fire and his mother is very glad. Then to Pat McAully. He is in bed and I think dying. He looks most awfully bad. That is consumption too. Then I had hardly any talk with anyone, so the war was not mentioned. Coming away from that house I fell in, as I did once before, with a woman in a khaki scarf. She stood at her door and began to talk. Oh yes it was her husband's scarf. He is in the Curragh Camp[18] now, he joined 'Kitchener's Army'. He was at Fermoy but moved to the Curragh. He came home on leave 'and oh I wish Kitchener would send them away, when it is that they may go any day you long they were gone.' From that to Delany's. He is not gone, his wife just cannot make him go, so he stays. His brother is wild to go back to the front. Mrs. D. never saw a man like him. He has one operation after another. He only wants to go back, and he soon will. The trouble was about his teeth. They were so knocked about by the shrapnel he was unable to bite and he could never have eaten soldier's biscuits, but now the operations have got them back into relation with each other and he can eat again, and will soon go back to the trenches, and Mrs. Delany's young brother is still at Fermoy, and as happy as possible. So then I went for a few minutes to old Ryan. He was greatly taken up with a clock which would not go. Its innards strewed the kitchen table, and he was very happy fitting them together again. So we only had time for a little general war gossip. But in seven houses there were five actively interested about the war.

The only funny thing about the departing Aberdeens was their title.[19] He was made a Marquis, and he took the title Aberdeen and Tara. Well we had as near a United Ireland as the Kaiser has made. Every sect, and party, set up such a yell of fury that he had to alter to Aberdeen and Temhair. Whether using the old Gaelic name made it any better I know not, but really the screams were rather fun. Among others, various sympathetic Scotch screamed with us, and said 'Oh how awful if some distinguished Irishman should choose Holyrood as his title.'

RS to DJS, 10 June 1915

I must tell you about the Belgian Band.[20] It was at the Hippodrome. It began at nine, and from 9 to 10.30 it got duller and duller, and more and more vulgar. There were some acrobats who professed to be Belgian refugees. They were rather horrible, though I was strangely thrilled when at the end of each dance on the tight rope, the girl said 'Voila.' Then came a magic lantern business, which was mixed with dancing in Japanese costume, and really rather pretty. Then came a cinematograph, shaking so that you could not look at it, and turning, as far as I could see in two or three glances, on someone who was turned out of the house while having his bath, and had to run about the streets dressed only in a bath towel.[21]

Then came acting, the chief character being drunk all through, and really at that point I had half a mind to leave. It was half past ten so while I was considering the matter the tipsy man reeled off to the asylum, and we were told the next piece would be the Belgian Band, 'and in introducing the Belgian Band, I wish to say every performer is either a wounded soldier, or a man too old to serve his King and Country' so up went the curtain and we applauded loudly, and the 22 bandsmen saluted us. They were as it were on the heads of a fort and cannon on each side and Rheims Cathedral as a Fond de scene with its red cross flying.[22] So we had a military march, and then another, and it was very sober sort of music and frightfully harrowing. It might have been my fevered fancy but I thought two or three of the players looked very melancholy. So the third piece began, and if the two first were sober it was downright dismal, and it got sadder, and sadder, and less and less tune, and more and more noise, and suddenly all the lights went out, the hall was quite dark, and the stage very nearly, and then the Cathedral began to glow, and blaze, and cannon fired, and shells shrieked, and you heard the bells ringing, in a wild sort of way as the draught from the burning caught them.

It was all quite badly staged and that only made it more awful, and I sat crying and crying. I felt if it went on I should die. It was all in combination with that horrible Blue Book, so gradually the noises left off, and the music came back, and the lights were turned up, and there was Rheims Cathedral on the fond de scene none the worse, and the element of absurdity only made the real tragedy more glaring. So then the Band rose to its feet, and began on a very familiar tune, and the audience rose likewise, and in came (as it were) a soldier, with the Russian flag, and stood 'at the salute' at one end, and then the Marseillaise and the flag appeared at the other end. And then a queer little tinkle and a Belgian flag came into the middle, so when we saw it we clapped like mad, and then came what rang in my ears as 'Heil dir im seige cranz' [Hail to the Victors] and a white ensign, and a Union Jack came, and supported the Belgian flag, and we all began clapping again and it was really a very effective tableau. Then all began to depart, and I waited a little to avoid the crowd, and as I waited I heard the voice of one making a speech, and it was partly military and partly not, so I looked about to see whence it came, and it was a man in the gallery haranguing a crowd of Tommies whom I had not observed before. So I said to someone are they wounded? And she said 'Oh no they are only the Ballykinler men, but they are leaving next week, so they were allowed this evening here.'[23] Well if there is a more awful sight in the world than Belgians, it is Tommies about to leave. So it was a very awful evening, and I felt very glad to have had it. One gets into such queer states. These awful dramatic things relieve one somehow. Someone said in one of the papers that he did hope we were all keeping diaries to tell our descendants what these fearful times are like. I think I am doing it to some small extent, with these weekly remarks.

The price of every blessed thing has gone up. I got a new hat the other day, and Mrs. Brennan told me it is next to impossible to get hats from France, and quite impossible to get them from Italy, the true home of straw hats, because the posts are so disorganised. Also to get good dying is impossible because all dyes worth mentioning come from Germany, and now do not come.

RS to DJS, 30 June 1915

I am breaking my heart over the Registration Bill.[24] Idiots! Lunatics! They have made registration compulsory in Great Britain and voluntary in Ireland. Who is it plays the fool like this? I am sending today's *Irish Times* so you can read about their asinine behaviour.

I went to Mrs. Cassidy's. There was Sarah, now married. Her man is a Protestant, and wants a Protestant prayer book. I am to get one, and Sarah will pay me for it. I wondered a little how they managed getting married, but did not ask. Perhaps he joined Rome for the day, people do sometimes, or perhaps she is going to turn Protestant. I gather she cares very little about religion in any shape or form. But poor thing she did look low about his going, and I made up some half larky message

'Give him my best wishes.' 'And' said Mrs. Cassidy, from the fireside, 'you're praying for him.' 'Yes yes' said I 'tell him that. Every day at the prayer meeting.' Isn't it nice the Romans thinking so much of the prayer meeting?

Then to Mrs. Rooney. She is very deaf, and was very low, today. 'It is an awful war. It is not lifting. If England should be beat what will come to us? It won't be a good government any more. We shall go down with England. I pray to the Mother of God England won't be beat. They will take all the boys for soldiers, and them not strong enough for soldiers, will have to make munitions.' 'Better go for soldiers' I yelled in her ear. 'Better be taken for soldiers than governed by the Germans.' 'Yes Yes' said Mrs. Rooney, quite cheerfully, 'much better. Look at Mrs. Armstrong next door. Her boy was shot dead a fortnight ago.' She felt it so much because he was not at the front. He was a despatch rider, and a sniper shot him. He had brought the letters, and had to go back with them. His mother spent up to £1 in masses, 2s. 6d. a mass. I am sure she was up to £1, all she had she said, and what has come of it?

'Look at our prisoners, all the good food they get from the King, and them Germans allows their prisoners nothing, they are starving. But (with a sudden gleam of satisfaction) after the war the Germans will have to pay England double for all that food the prisoners have eaten. I pray to the Queen of Heaven, and to her Son, England will win.' 'Oh yes surely we shall win.' 'Paddy says we are bound to win. I do not know. If England is beat down we will go.'

I really could not tell you how horrible it was. There was a grotesque element along with the tragic, which heightened it. It is so awful to have the war crashing in amongst old souls like that, and no doubt in all the fighting areas, there are plenty of shrewd old women saying 'Down we must go.'

RS to KS, 2 July 1915

[Registration Bill comment, c. 40 words] Did I tell you Mrs. Hughes has refused to have her husband's name on our prayer list? She says he is

prayed for already at the Chapel, and she is the only one to say that so far. He is a man that was chased off the Island in '12[25] and is now on the Agincourt.

RS to DJS, 21 July 1915

I think the war may last seven years. I do not in the least expect it to end sooner than the year after next, but I think Germany may at any moment go bankrupt, which I suppose would make peace necessary. *[Speculation on America's post-war role, c. 330 words.]*

The papers are horrible today. The Russians are barely holding Warsaw, which may fall at any minute. It seems the trouble is that they have not enough munitions. Apparently we ought to be supplying munitions to the rest of the Allies, I am not sure why. Even if Russia could make munitions it has this extraordinary railway system, one train runs on coal, another on gas, and another on wood and all the gauges are different. The idea is that when Russia's hash is settled Germany will turn to the west, and make another shot at Calais. Meanwhile there has been an anti-recruiting meeting in Dublin, I mean an anti-conscription meeting. The *Irish Times* does not advertise it much, but it was a hateful little meeting as far as it went, in a room of the Mansion House.[26] If conscription comes I shall regret the end of the recruiting meetings. They must be very wearisome to hold, but it is educating for the people. It is the universal appeal to all classes and parties which I have so long desired to see and which is now being put into force.

One evening I went along Brookfield Street (an exclusively Roman street) and there in a doorway stood a youth in khaki. So I said to myself 'James, that we pray for every evening.' And up I ran, and shook hands, and asked how he was, and he was much better, in fact he felt all right, and he had nearly gone to the front last week, only the doctor would not let him. However he quite thinks he is going out soon and I trust he may do so. He says the French are very good soldiers. 'They fight as well as we do.' He did not quite expect me to believe that, but he had become convinced of the amazing fact himself. So I said the Germans were brave too, and he got quite eager about that. 'Oh they were very brave, and quite sure they are right just as we are.' He said 'why had they got so far into France,' and I said perhaps because they were so well prepared for war, and he said 'We often talk about that in the trenches.' And I said it was very horrid that they had such a bad cause, and his eyes blazed, and he said in a shaking voice, 'I saw the Kaiser at King Edward's funeral, I was lining the road. If I had known what was coming I would have shot him.' And I said 'It would have been your last shot. You would hardly have fired another.' 'No no' said James 'but I would have done it.' There is something rather frightening in their feeling about the Kaiser. Old Kitty Madden is very feeble now, and she goes hobbling round the room, and he was mentioned and she turned round on me, her eyes as bright as James's were, and she said 'I would not give him a minute. Not one minute. If he were here I would kill him.' It was horrid she looked so awful. You know they regard the Kaiser as a murderer. It is so very awful the bodies go on being washed up from the Lusitania.[27] On Saturday July 17th three bodies were washed up in Kerry, two at Castlegregory near Tralee, and one at Glenbeigh. On Friday a body was washed up in the mouth of the Shannon, and next day, Saturday 17th a body was washed up in precisely the same place. Of course now the bodies are not to be recognised, but they can often be identified by watch chains, clothes and lifebelts. The Glenbeigh body was the only one they did not feel sure about, and at Ballyferiter a lifeboat came ashore in perfect order. Of course that was recognised at once as it was not injured. The country people look at it that all that is the Kaiser's own work, and I am not sure that they are wrong. From the Kaiser James and I got on again to the soldiers and he told me about Christmas Day. In the morning a shout came across to ask if, as it was Christmas, any of the British would meet the Germans half way between the trenches, and shake hands, and at first no one wanted to go, then some 'reckless' ones jumped out of the trench and the rest watched them, and had their loaded guns in their hands if anything had gone wrong. But Germans jumped out of their trench, and it became evident that it was all right, so then all the rest followed, and McKay went, and they shook hands all round, and the Germans had quantities of tobacco, plenty of warm gloves, and they gave them to the Rifles, and the Rifles gave tobacco, and whatever they could. They had all got Christmas presents on both sides. There were a few Germans who had been in London, and could speak English and they took the lead, and the rest stood and looked on and offered presents, and they chatted for about an hour, and then the officers called from the trench, and the Rifles had to go back, but neither side fired a shot for two whole days and nights. Then an English regiment came to relieve the Rifles, and McKay and the rest explained how nice the Germans had been, and begged they might not be shot at, but the English said Oh they would shoot when they got the chance. So after a while James McKay and the rest came back into the trench and McKay thought he never could shoot in that trench, but while he was thinking so a bullet hit his head and gave him a slight wound and he got angry 'I was angry and fired back'. I am not really sure that the Rifles asked the English not to shoot, but they told them what friends they had all become, and the English who I suppose had not seen the Germans, were quite indifferent, but is not all that an awful story? Well then one day a charge was ordered, and at the last moment it was countermanded, so the next day at the same hour it was ordered again, and just as the men were scrambling out of the trench to charge a voice from the other side called out 'Come on Royal Irish Rifles. Yous are twenty four hours late.' (McKay says they said 'Yous', he may not be accurate in that) and the Rifles were most awfully frightened.[28] It seemed like magic. However they charged, and got into the German trenches, but such numbers of Germans were there that they had to retire again, and McKay got all right out of the German trench, but while he was running back his own shot overtook him. He could not run, but crawled on his hands and knees, and when he was back in the trench he crawled for a mile to the clearing hospital and had his wound dressed and then he was sent home in a hospital ship with the Red Cross, and the Germans fired at it as it went. At least he thinks they did. I am to go back some day and have another 'crack' with him. It is nice when they talk like that, but it is also most appalling. You seem to see it all. You are keeping all these letters are you not? I have no other records of these warriors' tales, and I think one ought to try and preserve them. It seems due to the men. James said recruiting was all wrong, there ought to be none (a very common idea amongst the military, they think it is undignified), people should see the trenches, and I said 'What are you soldiers going to do with the trenches when the war is over? You have quite spoiled the fields for anything useful' and James said 'Oh but our last job will be filling them up.' I said 'Where do you put the earth when you dig them?' and he said, 'It makes a breastwork in front. It will be thrown in again at the end, but part of the trenches will always be kept. People will be curious to see what trenches are like.' I said 'What kind of a country is Flanders, and what parts have you seen?' I think he said he was at Vermeil, I am not quite sure about that, but he certainly was at Lavantie and he says all the country about there is very flat and there are, or ought to be, factory chimneys as in Belfast, but they have been destroyed.

When I told Ex. [mission worker, unidentified] about James McKay she got quite pale, and said 'Oh it's a risky business' and that is just what one feels. I forgot to say that the reason James crawled so vigorously was that he was awfully afraid of being taken prisoner. Mrs. Turner keeps heaps of pigeons, and she had to go on keeping them because they belong to Arthur. There were fifteen when Arthur left, and now there are thirty, and they are under police supervision. If they are taken to another house the police will have to be notified, and if a German landing takes place the police will come at once and wring all their necks. Are pigeons so intelligent as all that? Can they all in every place carry messages? And would all the messages they might carry be in favour of the Kaiser? [*Comment on America and Recruitment, c. 200 words.*]

RS to KS, 27 July 1915

As I look back on Carson's agitation now, it seems wilder and wilder, more and more like a dream. I imagine that it is utterly at an end, but of course I am not sure. It burst out once in a way I never could have believed possible had I not seen it. I suppose it might do so again. But at this moment it seems to me utterly mad, and utterly isolated, connecting with nothing either before or since. I am sure it was largely second sight: I think it would have been very strange if such a revolution as this war, had cast no shadow before. The whole Carson position rested on the Roman Catholics being rebels, and look how they are enlisting. Of course there is a rebellious section amongst them. They are going, to my great annoyance, to have a public burying of that brute O'Donovan Rossa, on 1st August, at which I fear a lot of trash may be talked.[29] But is that worse than the Welsh miners? There is a certain amount of treason in every country, and in free countries it speaks out and in non-free countries it plots.

RS to DJS, 3 August 1915

And this is no better. Croak! Croak! Croak! O'Donovan R. had a very huge grand funeral and the *Irish Times* in a very obscure corner and in nearly unreadable print referred to same. There were excursion trains from everywhere, and it was estimated that about 7,000 young men were present who should have been in the army, or who were of military age, and seemed in good health. But I was too low to read much about it and really I am not sure that beyond hurting one's feelings it matters so very much. Those young men were collected from all over Ireland, and I dare say a great many were feeding the army during the week, so beastly as the show was I expect it was more keeping up a silly custom than doing much fresh harm.

RS to DJS, 18 August 1915

[Comments on war losses and London air raids, c. 370 words.] The Registration has been an utter failure over here, not being compulsory. I enclose accounts of some hateful incidents to which it gave rise. The Unionists being so very spiteful and petty makes things worse and worse, because when the Home Rulers play the fool there is no balancing force anywhere. Here the papers were left by the police, with an assurance that you need not fill them up. Mrs. Halfpenny said the policeman had advised her not to fill her form, another woman who was there said Oh but the postman had told her it was better to fill it.

So a lively discussion ensued as to whether policeman or postman knew best. Presently I remarked that we should all be glad to help, and oh it was queer. Mrs. H. and the other woman and a girl who was in the room all shrieked in chorus. 'Oh but I would do anything for the Army — anything to help win — anything in the world if it was for the war — I would not care what they asked if it was to help win the war.' — Of course the Unionists want to get a lot of forms filled, that they may say how loyal they are, and the Home Rulers want not to fill forms because they want to say how independent and powerful they are and how unlike English people. It is all too silly. Bah — in Dublin men are registering but not women. Such a mess to make.

Here is my latest anecdote. Mrs. Conway said to the children 'Oh but I have a number of you.' Jemmy said 'Mother when I am big, I am going on the navy, and I will allow you a shilling a week. That won't be so bad will it?' And Willy said 'I am not going on the navy, I am going on the Connaught Rangers.' So I sat there laughing politely, and a little voice was uplifted, and it said 'I am going on the Germans.' 'Oh Maggie' said I to the only daughter 'the Germans!' 'Oh yes' said Mrs. Conway 'Maggie is a German. She plays German in all the games unless she plays nurse.' So I perceived that Maggie has a double role. Sometimes as the youngest she plays prisoner or corpse, and sometimes as the only girl she plays nurse.

RS to DJS, 26 October 1915

Sir Roger Casement is a Co. Antrim landlord, and a Home Ruler. [30] It seems that he took a leading part in exposing the stories about the Congo, and he was helped by Mr. Somebody Something now a leading English pacifist. Sir Roger spent his life abroad in the Civil Service, came home for a while and when the war broke out went to Germany, and got into great favour with the Kaiser. The other Home Rulers say he had a touch of the sun in foreign parts. Sir Horace [31] said of him 'Sir R.C. the last wild goose who has gone cackling to the Kaiser.' That is really all I know of him, and enough too to know of anybody. *[Speculation on end of war, c. 60 words.]*

RS to DJS, 4 November 1915

[Round-up on recruiting throughout Ireland, c. 2,000 words.] While
they are yet fresh in my mind here are war stories told by Jack to Mrs.
Halfpenny, and by her to me this day. On Xmas day he was at one of
the places where there were 'swaps' with Germans, and what the
Germans gave was chocolate, and cigars, and what the Rifles gave was
potted meat, the Germans had no meat, only bread and potatoes, and
such like. And at Christmas the Rifles (Royal Irish) were singing in the
trenches, all the songs they knew, and a voice called over from the
other trenches in English 'Can any of you dance?' and a Rifle called
back 'I can dance right well, but I won't you would be popping me,'
and the Germans said 'No we won't, you shall be safe,' and the Rifle
jumped up on the parapet, and he danced like anything, all the dances
he knew, and the Germans cheered and applauded. So one day the
Germans threw a note across 'It is our Colonel's birthday. Can you let
us have two hours truce to give a concert?' So we said 'Yes' and for
two hours the Germans gave a most beautiful concert, and all their
trench was illuminated, candles all along the parapet, and thanks to
the Rifles when the two hours ended. And one day a shout came
'What regiments are you?' 'Irish Rifles, Irish Fusiliers, Royal Irish
Regiment.' 'Well we are Bavarians, and when the Prussians relieve us
at 4 mind yourselves,' and after 4 there was a great bombarding. All
of which shows us we need not hate the Germans. *[Local news, c. 130
words.]*

RS to DJS, 23 November 1915

It goes on being most awfully harrowing about the recruiting. In
England it all looks very like compulsory service, but here instead of
having people in classes there is only the Lord Lieutenant's letter, and
it really will be beyond everything if Dillon[32] and Devlin[33] are right,
and if compulsion does not come to Ireland. It would mean that the
Irish regiments would be filled with Englishmen and that Englishmen
would save Ireland, and Ireland would be in a position of utter con-
tempt for evermore. Really I hardly like to put it in words, it weighs

on me like a formless ghost, because now a few days must decide it, but also I never do put it in words, and I try to forget such possible horrors. *[Discussion of war lectures given by RS, c. 380 words.]*

RS to DJS, 10 January 1916

The blow has fallen. Ireland is excluded from compulsory service. It is most awful. It is saying that Ireland is not a nation which can defend itself, but a sort of inferior kind of colony, which has to be taken care of by England and Scotland which are the real nations. It will lead to the Irish regiments being recruited by non-Irishmen, till all their Irish character is lost, it will make new occasions, and very serious ones, for the Protestants to say that the Romans are not loyal, and it will encourage empty talk about being anti-English, and being Sinn Feiners, amongst slackers who do not want the trouble of fighting. Indeed the people are being told that a patriotic Irishman ought to be a slacker. He assimilates himself to the English if he is too eager to fight. It is the worst political sorrow I ever had in my life, and the worst wrong I have yet seen done to Ireland. I think even Mr. Asquith would hardly have ventured on such a thing were he not growing very feeble. I think ten years in office, the last 18 months being during the war, is just too much, and he yields to Redmond, who is an utterly feeble creature, yielding to a minute handful of screaming Sinn Feiners, and to a great mass of crass rural greediness, and apathy. We have had 112,000 casualties at the Dardenelles. *[RS's response to KS's opinion on war, c. 500 words.]*

RS to DJS, 7 March 1916

[London air raids, c. 60 words.] Did I tell you we had a suicide last week, here in Albertville Drive. The funeral went past the kitchen window. She was a very decent woman, with a family, and it got on her mind about her sons being in the trenches, and one morning she went down early to get the breakfast, or some tea perhaps, before her daughters went to work, and they came down about 6 o'clock and there she lay dead in the kitchen with her throat cut. So Ex. had this awful news for Bridget[34] when she came, and B. said 'Oh yes. The very same has

just happened in our street.' So I am all for Cinemas and Socials now and anything to quiet people's nerves.

RS to KS, 11 March 1916

There was an all Cork Committee to get up a Patrick's Day Procession and the army offered to adorn the procession with some troops. Of course that was to make it a recruiting affair in a way. So some of the committee were very anxious to have troops, and some were very anxious not, and they voted, and the right side was voted out by two to one. And all the Unionists have withdrawn from the procession. The Sinn Fein people say they can raise 2,000 men of theirs to march, and the National Volunteers can raise 1,000. They are Redmond's men, and have supplied 300 recruits. But it will be intolerable if 3,000 young men march through the streets of Cork.

RS to KS, 17 March 1916

Redmond and Devlin and Sinn Fein may gabble away about exclusion, but really what the poor people feel is that if the Government wants them it will 'fetch' them, and if it does not want them why they need not bother. I said to a fine youth who came here with bread the other day, 'Why are you not in the Army?' and he said 'When the Govt. fetches me I will go with a heart and a half. But why should I go and leave my wife and unmarried loafers hanging around every corner?' I said 'Would you go if you were sure compulsion was coming?' and he said 'I would go tomorrow.' The Govt. is treating that man cruelly.

RS to KS, 14 April 1916

Ho! Ho! Such a rummy little sign of the times. A ring came and we opened, and there stood a mill girl gorgeous to behold, in her Sunday best carrying a tray of flags. You know the object I am sure. A tray in compartments, and flags of one kind and another, and you give what you please and there is no change. So I gave 1/- and took eight flags for eight allies, and she explained they were for getting comforts for the 16th Division. The 16th Division is the Nationalist counterpart to the

Ulster Division. So I said why only the 16th not the Ulster and she said there were too many to do all at once, and you see the English of that is that they have a Protestant collection for Protestant recruits one day, and a Roman collection for Roman recruits another and she was a Roman, and she had any amount of Union Jacks, also green flags with a crownless harp, and her tray was hung round her neck with a sort of twisted ribbon, red, white, blue and green and as I looked at her I said to myself 'The old order changeth,' and you know really this here war is doing a very great amount of good in Ireland, in spite of all the mistakes and failures. One gets so cross over this and over that but the good goes on all the time especially amongst the rising generation.

RS to DJS, 17 April 1916

I was most particularly glad to get that money for Short.[35] It will help to heal up a little breach which my out-spokenness partly caused with the Ulsterwomen's Gift Fund.[36] They send a parcel once a fortnight to every R. Irish Rifle's prisoner, and they are sending to Short. I got him first from the Irishwomen's Association in London, but they made me pay for the parcels, and as he is a local prisoner the gift fund here sends them gratis. Well both the London Association and the local one swear and vow they are utterly non-party and help all alike, so the one here hangs out in the Old Town Hall, and prints its subscription list only in Unionist papers, and the London people have just the same sort of aroma about them only on the other side. So I pointed out rather plainly to the people here what pigs they are only to advertise in the *Whig* and *Newsletter*[37] and they got decidedly shirty, and the one I was slanging — through a ticket collector's hole — said in tones of thunder that she was from the South, and I endeavoured to convey that that only made her party spirit the more blameable, and since then she has sent much wool to make special socks for Short, and I said in a note that I really was an ass to criticise so plainly for it left me with a terrible obligation to keep her. So then came your ten bob, and I have three left from the Magic Lanterns, and shall add two myself, and so pay for three of Short's parcels. That will put matters straight I think. But really the ten bob came in very pat. It is queer to see how hard party spirit dies. It is really very hard you know month after month it will soon be year after year to keep to the results of those weeks, well was it more like days of vision with which the war began.

RS to DJS, 25 April 1916

Oh but this is frightful. It went on till about 12.30 and no letters came, and no paper, and I felt a sort of creeping uneasiness. It was hateful, and I put on my hat and took some notes to the pillar, and there in one of the shops I saw a poster 'Cruiser off the Irish Coast — Sir Roger Casement imprisoned — ' and I felt in my pocket but there was no penny, and I ran in and borrowed one from Ex. and I flew to every shop in the neighbourhood, and the papers were all sold out, and the shops buzzing with the wildest rumours. 'The Sinn Feiners have blown up the Boyne Bridge. There has been a riot in Dublin — Ever so many people are shot — The Dublin mob has looted the Post Office — There was a Cruiser and a submarine — ' At last I lit upon an old man who seemed to have a head set on his shoulders. He told me that all the papers were sold out but that really I knew as much as if I had seen one, there is very little news, as all has been censored. All they say is that there was a cruiser, and a submarine, and it is quite certain that no Dublin papers are to be had in Belfast. I myself feel sceptical about the Boyne Bridge, the big one, I expect it is very well guarded, and I have a feeling that I have heard of other bridges called Boyne Bridge. I think it is not an uncommon name for Irish bridges. Also I am sceptical about the looting of the post office. Why should a mob loot a post office? Isn't it more attractive to loot shops? Also if someone hustled a postman might that not be called 'looting the General Post Office.' But about the rest I do not know what to think, Easter Tuesday is a bad day for anything like this. The people are hanging about, a good many doing nothing. The Island has had an Easter holiday, and here the streets are full of men who are hanging around, and inventing the details they cannot find out. I am sure it was like this in the old days when all news came this way. Now I am going out to see if I can find any place open where a paper might be to be had.

4.30 p.m. I have been to see the Shorts, the prisoner's sisters. Such nice girls, and I think the eldest not more than 17. So now I can send you his letter. The evening paper is not out, but Ex. has borrowed a *Newsletter* of this morning. It appears that the attempt to land arms and ammunition was made between the evenings of Maundy Thursday and Good Friday. A ship, indeed the ship, was sunk, and a number of prisoners were made, including Sir Roger Casement. So far good, and I should think the event was of no special importance.

[Comment on the alarm in Dublin, c. 250 words.] No doubt the *Newsletter* wants to make our flesh creep, but still I do think that it is very alarming coupled with the horrid fact that no news has come from Dublin today. You will I daresay know all that any of us are to know long before you get this, but I tell it all as it happens because one forgets so soon. Ex. has just been in — 5.10. The evening paper has arrived and it appears that Dublin is 'isolated', you cannot communicate with it by train, telegram, telephone or possibly by road. Soldiers, and business men are here, who came to spend Easter, and they cannot get away. You can go no further than Drogheda. I suppose at long last they are taking Sinn Fein seriously, and I suppose they are dealing with a conspiracy. That is all one can imagine, but I cannot tell you how awful it feels. All our letters come through Dublin, or at least all one cares to get, from Aasleagh,[38] or the South, or London, and the *Irish Times* comes from Dublin. To isolate the capital upsets everything in the queerest way, and I am sure if any way possible they will not tell the details, but the horrid report Ex. brought in was that some of the Irish Guards were shot in the streets there in a riot.

She said, and I quite agreed, not to tell that to Mary G.[39] because it might not be true. Someone said it on the authority of someone who came here in a motor, so it is rather vague, but I have told Mary about the isolation. She took it quite coolly, and perhaps did not realize how very odd it is. But she has both her sisters there, at Leeson Park. I think it must be a conspiracy, and they want to have the ringleaders in jail, and all the papers seized before the fellow ringleaders in the country know. I wonder who will be implicated? Hardly Johnny Redmond I should think. Poor beggar, but I am sorry for him. It is a most awful blow for Home Rule I am sure, whatever *it* may be. All soldiers in the North of Ireland are confined to barracks. I wonder will something be done away with now, and then a great outburst of Nationalist loyalty follow. It is Johnny's one chance if he cares for Home Rule. Oh dear I wish I knew what is going on and how can I write to Kate I should like to know? A while ago all the men on all the Belfast cross channel steamers were on strike. I dare say they are still, so one could only go to England via Dublin. I suppose if it were quite necessary to go there now one would go to Enniskillen — Ballyhaunis — Galway — Limerick — Cork, but what a state of affairs. I shall have to telegraph to Kate pretty soon if the isolation continues. And that is so horrid too. Why were a few hours not enough to arrest the men and to arrest the country leaders?

Friday 20th April [40]

Another of these queer days has ended. It is all so extraordinary one can hardly believe it is real. That meeting with Murrid was at midday on Wed. What happened next? Oh yes. I saw Mrs. Halfpenny in the afternoon, and Ryan, and the midday news was good. The disturbances were not spreading. Well then on Thursday we were still isolated, but we heard at 12 o'clock that the troops had occupied St. Stephen's Green, and before that at eight we heard that a gunboat had shelled Liberty Hall. In the afternoon, I saw Mrs. Halfpenny and I was in Brookfield Street. This morning at eight we were still isolated, and at twelve came the fearful news that the disturbances were spreading, particularly in the West. Martial Law was proclaimed all over Ireland I think yesterday evening, but all this news comes via London. We had no word direct from Dublin, and Charley Gorman was seen in the road to-day, as he did not go back to England last night. Mrs. Gorman declared a boat was going to Ardrossan. I do not believe it did. We hear to-day that Redmond and Carson have both very tremendously cursed the agitation and agitators. You know I am sorry for Sir E. I cannot believe he has not been a great deal more intimate with the Kaiser than was right in days before the war, and he must feel so awfully guilty now if he at all says to himself that it was he set the fashion of intriguing with Germany. For Redmond I feel in a way less sorry. His position is improved if he is now quite quit of Sinn Feiners. *[Local news, c. 200 words.]* The Romans are all loyal and solid to the last degree. Mrs. Donaldson says she is very unhappy. 'It is dreadful for the poor boys so easy led' and Mrs. Mickleman says she would not shoot any of them. 'No I would burn them. Burning is right for a man who raises a riot.' So from the extreme of pity for misguided ignorance up to the extreme of vindictive rage against such wickedness you hear every degree, but of sympathy not a syllable. I will repeat all I can remember of their sayings presently but not at this moment. Some of the people seem fearful of an outbreak of bigotry in Belfast. I trust we shall be spared that, but really it is all so wild one does not know what is going on, or what to look for next. One feels sort of bewildered by knowing so little and it is trying when one imagines that people in England know more. But perhaps that is only imagination. They may know no more than we do.

RS to DJS, 2 May 1916

I think now the disturbances are over, but I have as yet no comment to make on them. My mind is all a blank and I feel weeks must pass, or even months before I can make any remark. The shock is overwhelming. I had no idea that things had been allowed to reach such a pitch. Of course I knew there were no limits to Sinn Fein folly, or to the incapacity of the Government, and yet I did think there were limits to both. The seditious newspapers have been published again lately. I saw their ugly adv. in a queer little shop just below the Mater Hospital. I forget now what they all were, but sedition evidently. *[Accounts from Dublin, c. 400 words.]*

Bridget is here again to-day. She comes twice a week. She says the people are awful in her street, screaming out to her, and to Tommy, her husband, and to Paddy, her lodger, to go to Dublin to the Sinn Feiners. The most of the street is Protestant, and they yell specially at Paddy, and Tommy has told him not to stand at the door as he likes to do all the evening, also he told Bridget not to stand at the window, or a stone might be put through it. I took the G.W.[41] intercession paper down to Nelson to-day to be printed, but he says he is in a most awful upset. He hears that in Dublin reams of paper, great rolls with perhaps a mile of paper for the newspapers, were used as barricades, and the lead with which in printing you make spaces was melted into shot, and he thinks a large number of parish magazines, etc., which he is 'waiting on' were probably among the papers used for the barricading.

Same letter, 5 May

I think McBride was misinformed about those people being shot here[42], because yesterday we were officially told that three rebel leaders were shot in Dublin: Pearse[43], McDonagh[44] and Clark.[45] Pearse was a schoolmaster, not a National School, I do not think, and he was a member of the Irish Bar and an Englishman born in Dublin, and he was on the executive committee of the Gaelic League. McDonagh helped him at the school, and Clark was in penal servitude in the '80s for being mixed up in dynamite outrages. — I have now seen to-day's paper, and four more rebels are executed, and ever so many were condemned to death, and their sentences commuted to terms of penal servitude, and oh what do you think, amongst those sentenced to death, and actually to go to jail for ten years, is the name of George Irvine. It is so awful. I had a youth of that name in the Guild of Witness, for about a year, and he left the Guild because we prayed too much for the troops. I wonder is it the same? I should think likely.[46] Your letter of 9th April just arrived. I am going to answer it on another sheet. Here are two Dublin stories. Yesterday I went to the Northern Bank to change a cheque for Mary G. They told me to take it into the private room to be marked: 'All cheques on our Dublin branch must be marked now.' So I took it and the clerk told me that at the Dublin branch the Sinn Feiners had burrowed through the wall from the next house, but they got nothing, because money and valuables were all in the safe which they could not open. So I went on and called at the local office of the *Irish Times* to hear if that paper was yet to the fore. The man at the Bank was just bubbling over about the Sinn Feiners. We heard it on Wednesday 3rd 'by a message'. The boy at the I.T. office was bubbling over about the adventures in Westmoreland Street[47], news of which had just arrived. The Editor had fifty members of staff with him in the office when the row began on Monday. So they rolled 'great reels' of paper into the windows to be barricades, with furniture behind them, and they stayed in the office for four days and four nights, and one of them ventured out from time to time 'at the risk of his life' to get food. They had, or said they had a quarter of a million pounds worth of machinery on the premises, and they stayed to defend it, but they had no arms, and I think it was very brave. They slept on the tables, or where they could, and the military outside gave them leave to loot a large grocer's establishment opposite. It was deserted. One day the military at their request stopped a milk cart and forbade it to proceed, and a clerk flew out and brought all the milk it contained. It was the sniping made the streets so dangerous. On three days the paper could not be published, because all light was forbidden even a candle, and finally the boy put a copy of the dear creature in my hand, and I could have cried with pleasure to see its dirty face again. It was as the face of a friend, and a touch of common day in this nightmare. Alas dear I.T. It is a single sheet now, all its supply of paper having been used in the barricade, but news from Dublin is as I say the end of a nightmare.

RS to DJS, 10 May 1916

[Remarks on RS's disappointment over the Rising, c. 370 words.] Jack Halfpenny came safely home on Saturday night. It was a piece of unmixed and unalloyed good news, and James McKay is safe too, but all the soldiers who helped fight are moved out of Dublin, and others put in their places. The 3rd Battalion R. Irish Rifles is here for the moment, and Jack declares he is going to France with the next draught, which is as may be. Conway has been held up at home but is now I suppose in Galway. He is well from the accident but looks pulled down, being a Connaught Ranger he has to report himself in Galway. He was very angry over the rebel proclamation. 'They want to save further bloodshed.

Well if they do not want bloodshed, why did they begin? Did they think the troops were going to throw snowballs at them?' Did I tell you old Ryan's remark: 'They are a handful I have always said the Sinn Feiners are a handful. If Cork and Galway and Wexford had risen it would have been serious, but it is not serious; they are a handful.' Old McAlise who is a new old man, a sort of pendant to Ryan but less intelligent, says 'They are mad. They are utterly and entirely mad.' The most sympathetic are Mrs. Donaldson and Mrs. Halfpenny who are much concerned about the future of those who are shot. It seems that it is a widely spread article of belief that no one who is executed can ever go to Heaven! Mary Fegan told me that she had often heard Protestants say it, and she was sure it was true. Between a fear of the Sinn Feiners getting loose again, and a fear of their going to hell, Mrs. Halfpenny is much put about. Also she is afraid for Jimmy who is at the front though while he is there his prospects in the next world are very bright, for another article of faith which has come into great prominence lately is that if you die in war you are quite certain to go to heaven. Oh dear me. How very grotesque some of our notions are. Everyone is in a great hurry to have Sir Roger Casement put down. I have had to explain I do not know how many times that he must be tried first, and that it takes longer to try a conspirator for high treason, by the ordinary processes of law than to try a rebel taken red handed by Court Martial. The delay is not caused by Sir Roger being a gentleman, as some are inclined to think. Do you know it is so awful Countess Markievicz sentenced to death and now in penal servitude for life, was Miss Constance Gore-Booth daughter of Sir Wm. Gore-Booth of Lissadell, Co. Sligo, and she is about my age.[48] Mrs. McBride was Maud Gonne,[49] and is also a lady, and known to some of M.G.C.'s cousins, and Joseph Plunkett[50] is a son of Count Plunkett, whose antecedents I have yet to discover, but you see it is not a poor people's affair only by any means. I have not written any more for the Lord Mayor of Cork.[51] I feel hardly clear enough in the head yet, and besides we do not know about what might be coming respecting compulsion which would alter the tone of the articles if it came. *[RS's fears over her work, c. 60 words.]*

RS to KS, 26 May 1916

I am reading the Rebellion Inquiry. It makes me feel half mad myself to read of such insanity. It is like reading about a bad dream. Mr. Birrell went on just as people go on in a dream. I mean as one goes on oneself in a dream. An old person of my acquaintance whom I call No. 2 because I only know her number not her name, says 'There is something very, very bad in someone at the top.' And Mrs. Halfpenny says openly that he is in the pay of Germany. Do you think he can be possibly? I suppose not. Now how did Mrs. H. put it. 'Well I think Germany has them all in its pay.' 'Do you really think it has Mr. Birrell?' 'Well I do not know what to think' and I am sure I do not. Who ever heard of such a lunatic before? In a story one would say it was inartistic to make a man so very absurd.

RS to KS, 11 May 1916

I am feeling very ill again as you may imagine. Redmond is utterly mad I think. If he had gone in for compulsion now he might have quieted the country. Poor old thing. He has no idea how to rule men. He is just aimlessly going on with a sort of party talk, what he thinks will please 'Ireland'. I think his 'Ireland' is as imaginary a quantity as poor little Murrid's 'England'. My hopes are now all set on the Man of Destiny. I think such a one must be going to arise because the *Irish Times* has still such good articles. I send one for you to read. But it nearly passes endurance to have universal service everywhere else while the streets here are full of unmarried boys — Not the unmarried gone even. I think Redmond is sort of doting and his party is doting, and the boys here like the baker will go 'with a heart and a half' when they are 'fetched' and the soldiers' mothers are with Redmond.

I feel to have lost all interest in life. I heard about exclusion yesterday at 5 and it just seemed to snuff out the wish to live. Interest in the war I feel none. Let the Germans win; I care not whether it is they or we. I feel an utter blank.

RS to DJS, 12 May 1916

I think I did not mention Mrs. Owen. She is quite a new person on the gay military line. She says 'An *Irish* revolt. The best part of Ireland is at the Front.' She is a Crumlin Street Roman and her man has always been in the Army. To-day I was in Brookfield Street. Mrs. Cassidy is overwhelmed with misfortunes public and private, and says what was the use of the Dublin disturbances, what did they do? Why get themselves murdered and a great many other people too: no sense at all, it was all for nothing. Kitty Madden said she was afeared the lad in London[52] would get off, he was to be tried by three judges. They would not let him come back here, would they? He was from Ballymena, and no good person ever came from Ballymena. Well, if they do send him back here the people will lynch him. 'Bert says he won't come back. He will be shot.' 'Shooting is too good for him; I would cut him in little pieces. It was he began.' Old McAlise was rather tiresome and first he drew me into an argument and then I remembered his pulse. Before we came to politics he had told me that his was the fastest in Belfast, 190 in a minute, so I was rather alarmed to find myself in altercation with him and made a hurried retreat, and said the rebellion would do a great deal of good which seemed to calm him. Before we got to that point he had made one of those funny practical suggestions which jump out so oddly amongst the meanderings of the poor. 'They ought to give Home Rule. They ought to say "Go along, do the best you can", and pass a bill saying every young man must join the army.' I said of course every young man ought to serve, and I was sure the rank and file of the Sinn Feiners would make capital soldiers. 'There were boys among them fourteen years of age' said McAlise, 'and they went out in the morning saying "Mother I'll be in to dinner."' Then he rambled off into abuse of Carson as fons et origo [source and origin] of the whole thing and what a shame to allow gun running at Larne and shoot people for it in Dublin, and I began to point out that the people in Dublin were shot,[53] not because they gun ran, but because they hurted the soldiers and he said there was one law for one part of Ireland and another law for another, and the whole country ought to be disarmed and Mr. Asquith was doing his best and had as much bother as all the other Prime Ministers McAlise could remember. He would remember Gladstone, and Benjamin d'Israeli and in the last ten years Asquith had had as much bother. 'Yes. As much bother as Gladstone and d'Israeli had in all their lives.' 'Quite as much' so I began that Dillon ought not to have added to the trouble. (Did you see Dillon's speech? He said, inter alia, that the govt. might be damned glad if their troops fought as well in France as the Sinn Feiners did in Dublin. Was he sober?) McAlise said Dillon had wanted to defend his country, and hinder so many people being shot without trial, and I began to say they were not shot without trial, and in the middle I remembered his heart, and said good would come out of it at last, and he said a great deal of harm, and then good at last. Mrs. Cassidy is for wholesale executions. She says every Sinn Feiner should be shot as soon as he is taken. 'Shoot them, shoot them all.' Mrs. McAlise says, and so do others, that it is much worse than the war. She also says that they murdered the men who were fighting for them. But her James came safely to Belfast, I am thankful to say, and he had two hours at home and is now back to France to the trenches if he can, otherwise to the base, and Jack Halfpenny is still in town. She saw him on guard when she went down to work: she scrubs in the barracks.

RS to DJS 13 May 1916

I have this day seen Mrs. Lenehan and her sister, Cassie McNulty, also Mrs. Monaghan. Mrs. M. says the rebels have not been near her sweetie shop, which is really the chief matter, and she seems to care very little about them and their doings, but Cassie McNulty is awfully upset, and really cheered me up a little. Cassie has a great feeling about the King. It was she who, on the day that war was declared said she went about her work with a heavy heart: 'I am sure the King never thought his cousin would be so spiteful.' So to-day she said 'How could they do it when he has so much upon him? It was King George must have felt it when he heard, and Queen Mary too.' She is all for shooting every-body concerned. And when Mrs. Lenehan began how Sir Roger was not shot yet, Cassie said 'Oh no he did not come under the Act. It was so unlucky martial law was not proclaimed when they got him.' So I told about Countess Markievicz how she is about my age and grew up at Lissadell, Co. Sligo, and Cassie was most awfully shocked and said, 'She must be a mad headed sort of a woman.' Then we got on to these young boys, of whom apparently a great many are arrested, boys of fifteen and sixteen, and I said, 'Well if I were in charge of them, I should do like this. I should have each one separately out of his cell, and I should say, "Now listen to me. You are a very silly, naughty boy, and have been mixed up in bad mischief. If the King chose he might shoot you as a rebel. But you have a good King who does not want to shoot silly boys, but to see them grow into wise men. Now take your choice: will you go to prison for a long time, or will you take the oath of allegiance and join the Army? You won't get leave to go home to Ireland while the war lasts, but if you do well after the peace you will get a free pardon. And perhaps if you get the V.C. or even the D.S.O. you might get a pardon before the peace."' – 'And they would all go' said Cassie, 'they would all become good soldiers. Cannot you get it done?' So I said a great many people were thinking of something of the sort, and I was sure no one would be hard on people of sixteen. *[Copy of letter to Horace Plunkett regarding the above, c. 200 words.]*

RS to DJS, 28 November 1916

On Wed. and Thurs. I had the magic lantern for the R.C. children, and they came in with tickets and each ticket had to admit all the family naturally, and how many did you think came? Between eighty and ninety. What do you say to that? It makes me so happy. I do not mind being poor. I do not mind being tired, I do not mind *anything*. *That* is success. You know of course it may not last. Bigotry may arise, the house may be forbidden to them, quarrels, jealousies anything may come along, but the thing has been done. The people have had an example of what might be, if we all had common sense. I feel that whether Belfast heeds, or not, something has been done that cannot be undone, and some day somebody will heed.

Working with the lantern is better than going on committees. Oh, it was so funny on Wed. at the first lantern the children made an attempt to sing the 'Home Fires Burning', so then I said would they like to sing 'God Save the King', so they said they could not, and they did not know it, and so on and then some one started it, and a row of urchins in front suddenly (and quite correctly) began to roar out 'Send him victorious, happy and glorious, long to reign over us, God save the Pope.' So I assumed my most benevolent expression, and said, 'Yes, that is quite right, God save the Pope and the King. That is what we all wish' and if you could have seen the poor urchins. I laugh now when I recall their crestfallen faces. The show was over, and they thought it would be so jolly to have a row, and be kicked out with contumely. It was not at all the same to be very good little boys who had spoken for everyone.

RS to KS, 2 December 1916

Here is one of these tiresome incidents. I went up to the Roman streets this morning, and was pottering around calling here and there as I had things to say to the people. They were all just as usual, talking away over their illnesses, and the hard times, and so forth, and as I went I saw a crowd of children, and I stopped at a cottage door to see what they were looking at, and gradually they all came up to me and began to call out that they wanted 'tickets' and suddenly up came a female fury, and she began to roar that I was 'enticing the children', and the priests would not allow them to have my books, and I should take my books to the Shankill and not to this district. So I said 'Oh the priests know all about my books' — you know how I told them about the library when I first came to the house, in a letter which they never answered — and she continued to yell, and a crowd drew together as it does. Well luckily, I was quite near the Crumlin Road, so I strolled into it, and women were coming from the factories, and one of them took my part with fury, and tried to silence the yelling woman, and to one or two I said, 'What is wrong?' so they evidently had no idea, and I said 'Shall I get into the tram?' and one woman said 'Yes, you had better' quite kindly, so I got in and the matter ended. I think myself it was all the one woman, I think the children only wanted to bother me for tickets, and the one woman who looked to me as if she were fairly often drunk made a scene of it. Since then a Roman girl has come down for a book for her aunt, and her cousin wanted one too, and I said she must come back on Wednesday.

I guess really it did not amount to much. Idle children on a Sat. and I think it will settle itself, but it is rather a bore. I think it began with those children that I would not admit to the lantern. That roused some little jealousy, and I greatly fear it may be wiser to put off the women's Christmas party. They will be disappointed, but I shall explain to them that we cannot have boys in the garden ringing the bell, and spoiling our pleasure. Of course I know there is jealousy about me. The people all want to know me now, and all want to come here, and the only way will be for a time to ask none of them. It was queer about six months ago someone said to old Ryan that I was giving away 'tracts' and it was Mary G. who was giving them, strictly to Protestants only, and a while ago a girl said to a certain Cassie McAnally, who is a great friend of mine that I was meddling with people's religion. Cassie was in an awful rage and said nothing of the sort, she had known me for years and that was all lies. But those two remarks made me feel a smouldering jealousy amongst them. But also it all makes me feel how very wild and untaught they are, and how important my work for them is. That poor woman I think she was not drunk this morning, but she had a horrid face. I do not expect she is always sober by any means. For the next little while I shall restrict my visits to the early hours of the working days while the children are at school, and the majority of people working in the mills. I am sure my friends in the district fought a battle for me to-day. 'It is a shame for you children to be following her' — was what my champion said this morning, and more I think, which I did not hear, and she was quite unknown to me. You know it makes the sensible ones more sensible to have to stand up for me. It is really educating and good for them to have to keep the others in check.

Each of these flares up [sic] is a bore, but for so far from the days of Father Fox onwards, each flare up has been extinguished by Roman hands, and has left the people who put it out in a more enlightened state than they were in before.

RS to DJS, 7 December 1916

Yesterday I met Cassie McAnally in the road. She was the last person, or at least her mother was, that I was with before the row started on Sat. She is most unhappy about it, and she says the women are wild against me. They say I am lending books to turn the people from their faith, and they will put me out if ever I come to the street again, and they go round 'listening to each other's yarns' and they are all angry with her because she defends me, and her mother 'is awful annoyed' about it, and wanted Cassie to go down that night and tell me not to come back, but Cassie was afraid to go because they suspect her of being my friend, and she thought they would set upon her and I am not to come again until all is forgotten, but she will come and see me. I said well it was very tiresome of them just when a Roman Catholic lady in London had sent me a whole parcel of books from the Catholic Truth Society. 'You could not knock that into their heads with a hammer' said Cassie, 'They are awful ignorant.' So I said I would not come for a long time to that part of the district, and she was satisfied. Poor dears! They are the victims you know of utter ignorance, and of this silly social separation. But I am sure all the time the leaven is working. Some were on my side all the time, some will scream, and fume, and gradually calm down and know in their hearts that they behaved rather like idiots. It has come to my knowledge that when this happened last, ten years ago, Cassie's mother was one who was very much against me. I found that out by a chance remark to a third person. Cassie is so utterly sickened with the folly of the people, that I think she will take sides with the Protestants to her dying day. You see all this has followed on my getting an entrance onto Chatham Street, which is rather a low Roman street, and greatly needs to be enlightened. The poor Romans. It is tiresome for them to have anyone take quite as much interest in their improvement as I do. I do not wonder they resent it. I should do the same if anyone came so very much in earnest to civilise me. Cassie says I am not to give the party at Christmas to the RC women as they might come and then make a row, and as for the books lent in Chatham Street, I am to get them back by writing notes and asking for them, the notes to go by post. So isn't it well to have a friend at court? It will all come right with a little patience, and my position will be all the stronger. *[Reflections on RS's state of mind, c. 100 words.]*

RS to KS, 21 December 1916

[Reported conversation, c. 50 words.] As usual, I feel very low over our idiotic rulers. How can L.G. [Lloyd George] make such a fair sounding speech, and then gabble that gate about Ireland? He says truly that we are in a quagmire of suspicion. But who put us there? His party and himself. And how can he and Mr. Duke[54] go on saying that the atmosphere must improve before they can do anything? The atmosphere cannot improve till the government improves. That is what bothers me. L.G. and the Chief Sec. go on about confidence, and compromises, and what not and what is really wanted is government, strong executive government, the one thing private people, who happen to be loyal cannot give to their country. Now there was Dillon got up, and gave a long jaw about these interned Sinn Feiners, and Mr. Duke answered and apologised, and explained, and complimented everybody all round, and was longing to have the men out, and finally, after about a column of talk, said he would ask the Prime Minister about it to-day. He said Dillon was unkind, and the Prime Minister was ill, and was busy. My heart died within me as I waded through his meanderings. Here is what he ought to have said. 'I made an offer to the interned prisoners, that they should be released if they would give a promise to be loyal in future, they would not give such a promise, so I did not release them, and with my consent they never will be released, till they cease to be dangerous to the community. I think the time of the House need be no further occupied with this matter.'

Two sentences to that effect shouted (if possible in a good brogue) by a vigorous young man, would have cleared 'the atmosphere' they are all talking about. It would have been like a hand on the rudder of a drifting boat and a great wave of relief would have rolled through Ireland. Instead of that, wordy old Dillon chatters on one side, wordy old Duke on the other, amd between them I think they will probably soon get the men out, and yield a fresh victory to persistent and senseless nagging at the Government. There is fresh talk to-day in the paper of a conference to be summoned — this time independently of Government — to discuss the situation: all creeds and classes, that kind of thing.[55] But can any conference put spirit into the Government? You know really it is no excuse for them to say they are busy; the Chief Sec. has nothing else to do, only to govern Ireland. Let him do it, and all will be well.

RS to DJS, 27 February 1917

I feel that queer over the state of the country I am afraid…now shall I put this in words? Yes I will. It is silly to think you bring a thing on by speaking of it. I am most awfully afraid there will be more fighting before all is done. It is not just this or just that, it is a real wild revolutionary temper everywhere and all the bonds relaxed.

The government has deported 20 men and will give no reason for its action. Why did they let them out? They had most of them interned at Christmas and let them out, and now have to put them back again. Of course it is something that they do put them back. If there were a general election tomorrow everyone says that the Sinn Feiners would sweep the country. I suppose that means that they would get hold of a good lot of seats, and Redmond would reappear at Westminster with so few followers that he would not count.

Oh how I hate that man (Sir Edward Carson) going to the admiralty over to the showy job in London, and leaving the people he has upset to scramble as they can out of the mess he organized.[56] Having taken such serious steps as getting the arms and teaching the people to gabble about civil war, he ought to have stayed here and taken charge himself till the country really settles. No one could render the Empire a greater service than to help solidly in the settlement of Ireland. There must be other men for the admiralty.

I do think this fidgeting about, having men interned one day released the next, interned again or deported the day after is most awfully silly. It makes one feel that the Government does not know its own mind, and has no settled policy. A very uneasy feeling.

RS to DJS, 27 March 1917

The country is in an awful mess. The government is obsessed by the fear What will the allies say? What will democracy say if we oppress a small subject nationality? It is like the fuss made in 1881–82 about passing a coercion act.[57] It would be too awful to pass a coercion act, so Ireland went to the verge of civil war, and at last the coercion act was passed and Ireland settled in six weeks. Now again Ireland may be torn by factions, by rebels, by treason, towns may be burned, people killed in hundreds, property destroyed a million pounds worth at a time, but the government goes fiddling on about small nationalities, and what everybody is going to say.

RS to KS, 6 April 1917

Miss Malcolmson was talking last night about Arthur Kavanagh the limbless man.[58] She told me how he was an MP till the election of 1885 'and then my father knew his seat was most unsafe, and Mr. Kavanagh said "But Malcolmson they have all promised" and my father said "Yes but they have the ballot."' So the day came and Mr. K was nowhere, utterly at the bottom of the poll 'well but it was not only that. Two nights later they burnt him in effigy at his own gate, they made a figure without arms or legs and burned it. It was a firebrand of a priest made them do it, and Mr. Kavanagh was utterly broken hearted. He let his house and never lived there again. They owed him so much and he thought they were devoted to him.' 'The silly man' said I 'Why did he not know them as your father did? And why did he not go about the village very kind and friendly. In a week they would have been in despair at what they had done.' I felt half scared at speaking like that of a man who had been her friend more or less, and who certainly had sustained a very brutal insult. Well she looked at me and her whole expression was radiant. She felt as if a light had broken in, and she said 'There were some of them who were in despair as it was, and the priest who organized it was removed. He had acted outrageously, his own superiors could not stand it. But Mr. Kavanagh expected gratitude from those people.' 'He was quite wrong' said I 'he ought to have said to himself that landlords have done a power of harm in Ireland, and the Irish Church has done a power of harm in Ireland, and it is for us of this generation to expiate it. If he had looked at it that way he would have put up with the pain they gave him.' And then I told how often the people had tried to get me out of the streets, calling me a souper, and how I never did anything but laugh. And then I said I had learned that from Sir Horace Plunkett who always laughed, and was good tempered, always good tempered when the poor people tried to insult him, and how they had had to give up insulting him when they found that it only made him chaff them. That was much better than Queen Victoria staying out of Ireland for 40 years because the Fenians broke up a meeting which was held to erect a memorial to her (prosy old prig of a) husband. How could she have played straight into the hands of the Fenians? But Sir Horace's whole work is based on repentance.

RS to KS, 31 May 1917

I am told the UVF districts are full of arms, and how many the Sinn Feiners have is not generally known, but I suppose they have some. What makes 'compromises' and 'settlements' and so forth seem so hollow is that a very cowardly Government is treating with armed rebels, instead of punishing them and making them lay down their arms and become decent citizens. Really I hardly wonder that people turn Sinn Feiners. The Government is *such* an object. I think all four volunteer associations ought to be proclaimed in one notice in alphabetical order.

The associations known as

> Dublin citizen army
> Irish national volunteers
> Sinn Fein or Irish volunteers
> Ulster volunteer force

That would show that it was not a party measure, but a real resumption of power by the government, and no one could scream very loud because their enemies would be gone as well as their friends.

From the very beginning I thought the Ulster Volunteers dangerous rebels and told them so. When the rebellion came I thought it was the first fruits of Carson's teaching, and I think so still, not the whole harvest but the first fruits. But what am I to do now when, instead of being in the least repentant for having been in rebellion, or at least risen towards rebellion, and started a state of anarchy in Ireland which led to the burning of Sackville Street etc. — they are very crowing and triumphant and boastful. *[Reported conversation with Unionist supporter, c. 550 words.]*

RS to KS, 8 June 1917

Yes I do speak plainly. I am a bit afraid of going mad myself. There is something infectious in the surrounding lunacy. I should not join any of the existing parties, but I should be as mad as any of them. I often feel a perfect passion of hatred against England, a longing to read of German victories, and other sensations equally apart from reality which I cannot at the moment recall. *[Sinn Fein meeting, c. 80 words.]*

I think the Roman priests are very pathetic. They have the erroneous, but very common idea that you can have a good rule which will do always and save further trouble. They are taught that they are Catholic priests, the leaders, guides, teachers of all the world, they must minister to the faithful few, and beware of the heretics, and all that is quite out of date, and it ends in keeping them in a horrid little pen of their own while the great world rolls past them and while even the devout RC poor go ahead of them in most directions. And many of them have quite enough common sense to know their own limitations. They know they are ignorant and they vaguely feel their own world a very small one. I think they have the feeling that Protestants know everything, and can do everything and you must keep cursing them all the time or they will sweep you right away and none of you will be left.

RS to DJS, 19 June 1917

Oh dear it is all very horrible. A great wrong left unrighted. It is Jimmy Halfpenny. He was killed in action on June 7 and they heard it today. It has given me a great shock. I had so set my heart on his getting some distinction, and some public recognition in Belfast. I went to the house to ask them to the tea party. The last time I was there to ask them to a tea party was on Xmas eve 1915. I recall it as one of the last happy days of life. Exclusion came on January 5. I went in with the invitation and Mrs. H. gave a shriek of joy and said 'See whom I have here.' And there was a huge young man in karkhi [khaki], eating tinned salmon for his dinner, because it was Friday, and a fast in itself as well. And I recalling the weedy boy who got knocked about at the Island[59] did not recognize him, but from her shrieks I gathered who he was. And today they were all sitting round the room, and she shrieked again at the sight of me, and it all came back. I think she did not want me in, but I went in, and it was better. Someone muttered 'Jimmy killed' and I felt half stunned and as if I could not leave. They had an official letter from the War Office, and a message from the King and Queen. That makes it quite sure, and now Belfast cannot make that atonement.

More than 200 Sinn Fein prisoners were returned to Ireland on Monday. The whole lot are out, Countess Markievicz and everybody. Ever so many were sentenced to death, and had had their sentences commuted to penal servitude for life, twenty years, ten years etc. Now every jack man is out. Miss Malcolmson says 'I do not think the amnesty can do any good. Many of them are actual murderers, and all in intention.' That is what I think, and what we all think. I feel sure there will be more fighting.

I am wondering how it would have been if instead of allowing those people to land Sir Bryan Mahon had either sent them straight back to England, or had held the quay with soldiers, and put the whole of them back in jail on his own responsibility.[60] I suppose even the cabinet would have recalled him but he might have refused to leave, and just have held Ireland for 'the King'. Not for George Frederick, who might have stopped the amnesty, but for 'the King', that ideal personage who ought to be enforcing righteous laws. Such a person exists ideally though not actually, and I think that a time may come when it really will be necessary for the army to interfere and save Ireland from Parliament. I cannot describe to you the utterly disorganized feeling of everything.

RS to DJS, 17 July 1917

[Report of political argument, c. 500 words.] Now here is a story, and I do not know how far it is true. The Rev. W. Browne of St Mary's told it to me.[61] Willy Redmond was nearly sixty, and at Messines his Colonel said Major Redmond you are to stay at the back, and the younger men are to lead the charge.[62] So Major Redmond, in a most unmilitary spirit, said 'Do please let me be in the charge, I can never again look the men in the face if I am not.' The Colonel said 'For one hour only.' So Redmond took the place he wanted, and he was hit in the arm and in the leg, and they were small wounds but they brought on shock and collapse. An Ulster division ambulance took him to the back to a dressing station, and there they found a chaplain, lately curate of Holywood and C. of Ireland. He took messages which Redmond was able to send, and then Redmond said 'Do you think there is any hope for a man like me? I have always tried to do my duty.' The Chaplain said 'I pointed him to Christ' and Redmond said 'I have always had a great respect for your church'. By that time they had him bandaged and sent on to the base, and a Roman priest was found who gave him extreme unction while he was unconscious. He never spoke except to the first chaplain. An odd part of it was that the chaplain's name was Redmond, Rev. J. Redmond of Holywood.[63]

RS to DJS, 6 September 1917

I do wonder if by any miracle that Convention is going to do any good. Sir Horace is that delighted with it, the poor man! I do so wonder is it possible that the rebellion gave people such a fright that now they are really going to try and make up a reasonable plan. If they do it will make the Covenant seem rather nonsense. Oh dear it would be a lightening of the skies if they could agree on anything tolerable. There have been several court martials for illegal drilling and for exciting disaffection. I read about six or seven. May they be the first of many.

RS to DJS, 24 September 1917

In the Convention I now feel no hope at all. Of course I never thought it would or could settle the country. I think it may part in peace and civility, and I think it may be the means of introducing some new ideas which may slowly penetrate a few thick skulls. L.G. has, I do believe, disqualified himself for governing firmly, but he is very clever. The Convention has staved a crisis off, he may think of some other clever dodge, and go on staving off and staving off till times somehow improve. Lloyd George is a dreamer, a dreamer of the people, and as far as the war goes his dreams have led him on to reality, but in Ireland they have led him into hopeless error. He does not understand backward country peasants. His vision is all for the middle classes, and so he gets on very well in the England of the present day.

The Government does not want to know about Ireland. They want to manage Ireland, to please this person and that person, to say one thing to the labour members, and another thing to the Irish Americans, and to produce such an effect in S. Africa, and do such a deal in Canada and for Ireland itself they do not care. That is my deliberate opinion. They offered four seats in the Convention to Sinn Fein, Sinn Fein refused, but it is not thanks to the Government that murderers and avowed rebels are not sitting there at this instant. *[More comment on the Convention, c. 280 words.]*

RS to DJS, 2 October 1917

[London air raids, c. 350 words.] As for Ireland the good is about the Convention, the bad is about a brute called Thomas Ashe who hunger struck, and died.[64] He was a Sinn Fein convict, and he was sentenced for life after the rebellion, and let out last June. A few days ago, during that temporary show of energy, he was put in jail for a year under DORA[65] for illegal drilling I think. He hunger struck in order to be treated as a political prisoner, and he died. He lay in state in the hospital dressed in a Sinn Fein volunteer uniform, though uniforms other than the King's are forbidden, two men in the same costume stood on guard, and 15,000 people came to see him (I give the figure from memory). Then he was moved to a Church (i.e. a Chapel) then to the city hall. Marching in military formation is forbidden, but Sinn Fein volunteers etc. managed to get in three marchings after the coffin till it was

finally underground at Glasnevin. Now the Government has made a change about the other prisoners which is understood to make them political prisoners, and some are discharged so Ashe has won very completely. The English do not attend to all this, but will not blame the Government for the next rebellion. If these people are to be political prisoners now it would really have been better not to have shut them up. They are only being made more and more lawless, and more and more contemptuous of the British cabinet.

The Convention seems to be going on very happily. Dear Sir Horace always cheers me for the moment, but as to what the permanent value of their proceedings will be I really cannot form a guess. K. is sending you the papers containing some articles called *The Ferment of Revolution*. I thought them most interesting. I have no idea how far they are true, but the whole thing as I read it, suggests to me that Sinn Fein may be only the Irish development of a spirit of revolution spreading through the world.

K. thinks that people in England as far as they remember the rebellion (which of course most of them do not at all) think of it as a Belfast riot. It was a riot actually, a bad armed riot which it took a week to stop, but in spirit it was not rioting at all it was revolution. Real anarchy aiming at a general overthrow of the existing order, not an outburst of spite and mischief as a riot is. [*Comments on international social unrest, c. 190 words.*]

RS to KS, 23 November 1917

There is no special news. I send various accounts of the spreading of Sinn Fein. You see it is now being well and thoroughly organized all over everywhere. Lord Wimborne made a most odd speech.[66] He says he is afraid to arrest de Valera lest there should be an outcry in Ireland which would prejudice the Convention. He thinks [it] very likely the Convention will fail in any case, but if it does no more it will bring about a definite statement of differences, and that will be a great gain. He says that whatever happens the Government cannot and will not tolerate drilling, which is 'political opinion backed by physical force, and inconsistent with the first rights of civilised communities'. I repeated that to Mrs. MacIntosh and she said 'He might have left that out. Where Mary is in Co. Clare, at Kilkee, they are drilling every day' and you can see by the extracts I send from the *Irish Times* that Kilkee is not peculiar in that. One of the duties of a Government is to be supreme, and to tolerate no fancy governments. When it says openly like that it is afraid of the fancy Government which stands at its elbow inviting the allegiance of the citizens it has in practice abdicated.

RS to DJS, 7 January 1918

There is a Sinn Fein meeting held about once a fortnight in St Mary's Hall. I am not sure to whom the hall belongs, some Roman Catholic body, evidently afraid to refuse Sinn Fein. The Turners say that the Sinn Feiners asked for the hall up here at Ardoyn, and the Holy Fathers refused. A party of Sinn Feiners came into the Chapel, and sat round the door talking and making a great noise. One of the Fathers went down and told them to come up and sit in front, and they all jumped up and ran out of the Chapel, and the Father said 'Go along. The Church will do very well without you.' At St Mary's Hall it is so awful. They had a meeting addressed by Countess Markievicz, a second organized by Cumaun na Maun [Cumann na mBan], now one to be addressed by Alice Milligan. She is a Churchwoman, they choose Churchwomen for this place I believe.[67] She is older than I am I should guess, so she has had time to learn more sense than to stuff the people's ears with cram about Irish republics.

Here is the advertisement:

Sinn Fein

Belfast Executive

Irishmen and Irishwomen of all creeds and classes

Don't miss the

POPULAR LECTURE

to be delivered by

MISS ALICE MILLIGAN

in St Mary's Hall
on Thursday 3 Jan at 8pm entitled
BELFAST IN THE MAKING
Will Belfast be a stumbling block in the setting up of an Irish Repub-
lic? Or will it clamour to be allowed in?
Come and hear
Popular prices 6d and 3d
EDUCATE THAT YOU MAY BE FREE

I stood making a copy of this and up came two women and a girl, in shawls, and began to read it. I said 'are you going to that lecture?' Oh yes they would like to go, they thought they would go. Did they want an Irish republic? Oh yes, anything for Ireland . . . Of course, certainly, anything for Ireland. But would a republic be good for Ireland? . . . and then I felt too much stirred to go on being cautious, and I said 'You know an Irish republic means bloodshed. It means ever so many people being killed. What good came of the bloodshed in Dublin?' and the girl muttered to herself 'none whatever', but one of the women said 'Oh there must have been some good. People would not die unless they thought they would do some good. And (a sudden pleasure lit up her face as of one who remembers the answer to a riddle) they stopped con-scription. Oh yes, they stopped conscription.' I said 'But is it a good thing not to have conscription? Englishmen are dying for Ireland. Is that right?' She said 'I would not trust England the length of the street' and my heart sank. To what purpose to argue with a woman to whom the most elementary processes of thought are unknown? Then the other woman said 'I must go. I have the dinner to get' and the others cried 'The dinner. The dinner' and I said 'Oh yes. The dinner is much more pressing than the Irish Republic' and they folded their shawls over their heads and ran like hares. *[Comments on conscription, c. 100 words.]*

RS to KS, 14 February 1918

Anyone who tries to establish any respect for law will have their work cut out. The country is frightfully demoralised and lawless. There are raids for arms continually, and prisoners rescued from the police, and illegal uniforms and all this crazy Sinn Fein business. Orders are issued on all sorts of matters in the name of the Irish Republic. They have now given some order about compulsory tillage, and in a few places it is being carried out. Of course that only means some sort of bargain between a Sinn Fein committee and a few farmers, but is very horrid. And at S. Armagh, did I tell you? there were any number of motors, and some of the chauffeurs were asked where they got the licenses for petrol, and they showed permits signed on behalf of the republic, and the police took no further steps. The Ulster Volunteers have any amount of arms, and the Government knows that these arms are in the hands of private people, and they do nothing.

RS to DJS, 18 February 1918

I have been much interrupted in this letter as I have been directing some painting in the back yard being done by James McKay. It is so awfully sad to see these discharged boys hanging about unable to work, wrecks in the full tide of youth. He has his right hand stiff and useless, and also a bullet in his liver which they cannot get out. He has done the painting quite nicely. I am going to try and get him an allotment. He is getting 18 and 3d a week, and a sound man in Belfast now often earns two or three pounds at the Island. He is 27 or 28.

I hear that Dublin is full of stories told by people of all parties of the horrible things the soldiers did during the rebellion. I am quite sure that if Sinn Fein had prevailed we should before now have come to a guillotine and a reign of terror. It was no doubt better to do those things than to let the rebellion go on. But all the same those stories about soldiers executing innocent people are very horrid, and having them widely told does a great deal of harm.

RS to KS, 28 February 1918

It appears to me from the quotation given in the *Irish Times* of what the 'London *Times*' says, that the London *Times* is taking the state of Ireland very coolly, or else the *Irish Times* is lying freely.

Sinn Fein is really beginning to take hold now. Boys sing when brought into court to be tried, and wear their caps. When told to be quiet they say that the magistrate represents an alien country, and that England has no jurisdiction in Ireland. That is quite new. The ordinary rowdy boy did not know it till about last week. And it rather frightens me when the Dublin correspondent of the *Times* says that 'Mr Duke only returned on Saturday, and we cannot expect immediate results from his efforts to restore order.' A pretty state of things when 'measures to restore order' are necessary because the Chief Secretary spends a few days in London.

Did you read about the girl whose brother left a German sword at home? He took it from the German himself, and left it hanging on the wall. One night her father was out, and disguised men broke in raiding for arms. She got hold of the sword, and the raiders told her to give it up. She would not. One of the raiders pointed a pistol at her and said 'I am going to shoot'. She said 'Shoot away'. He said 'One Two....' and then put down the pistol and she kept her sword, but was rather hurt in the struggle. Her sister tried to go to the yard for the dogs, but the men hindered her.

At Ennis no one is allowed by the police to be in the streets after 6 pm, because now Clare is 'proclaimed'.[68] The paper says that evidently in Clare the illegal ploughing and cattle driving are organized. They break out in places so very remote from one another, that the police spend their whole time on the road, running from one scene of disorder to another, and are allowed to do nothing when they get there. Really there is nothing makes me more uneasy about the war than this horrid suppressed insurrection.

RS to DJS, 9 April 1918

On Wednesday April 3rd I went down to 322 Mill Street to see about the petition.[69] To outward seeming 322 Mill Street is a small shop about three minutes walk from the Bank Buildings, and the very heart of the town, but up a side street. In the window are rebel songs, post cards etc. and bunches of rosaries in yellow, green and white beads. In the post cards we see Patrick Pearse and so forth falling at the feet of the country, which now accepts them as martyrs, and we see everywhere a personified Ireland escaping from the tyranny and agelong oppression of a personified England.

I went in and asked a youth of about 25, and a salesman of perhaps fifty, if I could see the petition. I was told I could. Did I want to sign? No only to look at it. So it was produced, a little stiff book with blank pages for the signatures, and the petition on the first page. The petition itself is very short, and is reproduced in various languages. It says as far as I can remember that the nations of the world are asked to establish Ireland as an independent state. While I turned it over the two men seemed to be speaking of the difficulty of stocking shops with tobacco. Presently I said 'You seem to be great friends of the Germans here' for the petition stood first in Irish, then in German, then in French, then in various other languages ending with English. I said 'On what principle are these languages arranged?' The shopman said he did not know. I would not look round but I heard a sniggering going on behind me about 'Ireland at the top, and England at the bottom.' I said 'Proper diplomatic precedence is found by translating all the names into French, and then taking the alphabetical order.' I began to apply this test, which does of course give German a high place. Gradually I became aware that the younger tobacconist was looking at me very respectfully. I perceived with wonder that my easy talk of diplomatic precedence, and translation into French, had had the desired effect, and had really impressed the youth with the idea that he found himself in very grand company. I walked all round the shop with a word here and there, and looked at all the sedition, likewise at four other boys who dropped in and listened. They were very young, 18 or even less, to 20. It was the Wednesday after Easter, and there was a football match to which I felt sure they were all going. The whole week is a holiday here. My remarks were addressed to the tobacconist, but my heart was so torn for the boys that I felt I was not at my best as an upholder of argument.

I asked him what was England? Come to that what was Ireland? 'Ireland means everyone born in Ireland of Irish parents.' 'What was the

House of Commons? English or Irish?' 'Oh English of course'. 'And 103 men in it born in Ireland of Irish parents'. 'Yes but not real Irishmen, only pretending.' 'Was Patrick Pearse an Irishman?' 'Oh yes indeed.' 'But he was born in Ireland of English parents.' 'Oh well he died for his country, and he moved Ireland.' 'Ah there now. Was the tobacconist thinking of the facts at all? Was he not just giving the name of "Irish" to anyone he happened to like? Really now and truly was not he fancying a wee bit?' And with that I left because it was the moment to leave. If you say a word too much it is so fatal. It was not as concise as that, but those were our arguments and our words, and it was interrupted by my wandering about and looking at all the trash in the shop. The old shopman was more than pleasant. He was so gracious that all that day I had hazy visions of going back, and getting him to introduce me to some of those poor youths, and getting some of them to come and borrow books and I do not know what all.

Next day I told the whole story at tea at the Ewarts, and the girls were most awfully taken with the idea of going to the shop and buying rebel rosaries, but as I walked home I felt that the girls must not go there. Why not? Gradually it all got clear. The place is no shop at all. The old man never asked me to buy, and I must have been there a quarter of an hour. In these days a small shop could not sell all that printed matter and make a profit. It came on me all in a minute, that the old man is paid a fixed salary, that the shop is really just a Sinn Fein committee room probably financed from Germany. Likely all the things were printed in Germany and sent over, anyway the man is a German agent I feel no doubt whatever about that, and I wrote and said all that to Alice Ewart, and I hope she did not go there. I shall not go again. I do not wish to make the beastly little hole look respectable. But I am going to the other Sinn Fein shop this afternoon, and will send Herbert a good packet of treason which I shall buy as a witness against the government.[70]

On Saturday I felt mortal tired, and it is my day to see the Romans. I thought I was too tired to go, but then I said 'No. It may be our last peaceable Saturday. I shall go.' So I went and paid 16 visits, and it was all as nice as nice. The people all very affectionate and just as usual. The last house was Mrs. Delany's. She it was who persuaded her husband not to go to war, as he wished, because there is such a poor provision for widows. The separation money would have been all right, but if Peter had been killed what could she do with so many children?

This last Saturday she had in her house a most insufferable youth. He had Sinn Feiner written large all over him. He was rather well dressed, and stood in a most superior attitude, looking on with a very patronising smile while we talked. It is quite new to meet Sinn Feiners so easily. Six months ago I should as soon have looked for a Sinn Feiner in a Nationalist cottage, as I should have looked for him in a lady's drawingroom. Almost less soon because of course some silly drawingrooms do grow Sinn Feiners.

Gradually I drew this youth into talk. He was quite old for a Sinn Feiner, about 21. I will repeat the substance of what we said but it looks more convincing on paper than it sounded to me in saying it. Thinking it over afterwards one can only remember the bones of the argument, and set out side by side the bones make a better show than the talk did. There was a modesty in this boy when you got at it, and I am not sure that really he was not the best I have met. He said that in nine months England would be quite beaten and destroyed by Germany, and Ireland would be Germany's friend and quite secure. 'And' said I 'every man conscripted for the Kaiser.' 'Oh no Irishmen will never fight for the Kaiser.' He really did imagine that the friendship would be between two equal powers. He told me how Pearse loved Ireland. I said 'No. If he had truly loved Ireland he would not have gone out without military training to fight an army.' 'But what did Pearse do.' It is so horrid, as they begin on the theme whose watchwords they have learned their whole manner changes. They adopt a very affected voice, a sort of theatrical rant, the Ulster Volunteers and all do it. It is like saying your part in a very vulgar badly acted play. Imagine therefore a would be dramatic voice and manner as the boy screamed out 'And what did Pearse do? With his men he kept the British army, the great British army, the greatest in the world with its six million men, he held it for a fortnight.'

'No' said I speaking very softly and calmly 'Pearse went out on Monday, and he surrendered on Saturday. That is not a fortnight, it is not even a week. The soldiers were a long time putting down the riot, for it was only a riot from their point of view, and Dublin was home to them. It was their own place. They did not want to break the water mains, or to interfere with the gas. You have to fight very gently putting down a riot in your own town.' And the poor lad looked at me quite simply, and dropped all his heroics and said 'Yes it was their own.' I told him he did not really understand what he was talking about. He had read no history. And he said Oh yes he had read Sullivan's history of Ireland and I said Sullivan was very slight. He should read Lecky, and it did seem so dreadful to think of a man who wanted to read history, and had no one to tell him how to do it.[71] And he said he had no time he had his living to earn, and I said well if a man had really to give all his time to earning his living than he should not take a side in politics for he was unable to know anything about them. And by that time he was looking at me in a wistful sort of way. For the moment he wanted me to teach him, because he felt that I was much older, and quite a good bit wiser than he was. I daresay the impression went off directly but it was there. I am going to take some books for him up to Mrs. Delany, but poor lad, he ought to join up next week and leave Belfast. If they had sent him two years ago he would either have died honourably at the front, or he would be a fine loyal soldier getting on well in the army.

RS to KS, 18 April 1918

I am going to send this off now. I understand that conscription will not be enforced till after Home Rule passes, so Sinn Fein wins.[72] I thought it would. I had no real hope after that meeting on Sunday. To allow the flag, and the cheering was in fact to yield everything.

They all think over here that the Cabinet has quite yielded. The rent agent called here today and I said something about it, and he grinned, and said 'Oh conscription is dead.' He is a Unionist and a Protestant. You see by the placards that Sinn Fein boasts of having killed it. But now the great thing is to get the credit of having stopped an unpopular measure. The RC Bishops are calling out the most insane things, the people are to meet and pray against this inhuman cruelty, and I do not know what all, the greatest stuff you can imagine. There are quite a number of them saying well at this moment they do not advise armed resistance, no on the whole not, anyway till we see what passive resistance does. They are suggesting rebellion in the plainest terms, because they feel that if they do not Sinn Fein will take the whole credit for frightening the Cabinet. And the Nationalists, as you see, are openly allaying themselves with Sinn Fein, and I believe in the same spirit. There is to be a by election somewhere, and as a protest against conscription Dillon will not run a candidate, and there are to be allied meetings of nationalists, and Sinn Feiners to protest. Devlin is said to have recruited 6000 men from the Ancient Order of Hibernians and the National Volunteers in the beginning of the war, and now he is as bad as any of them. I think that he and others are terribly afraid of not standing well with the powers that are to be, and so they join what they think is the rising sun of Sinn Fein. And Sinn Fein is Germany. It is partly what I told you about the shops that makes me so sure about the German influence, partly the unlimited command of money, and of things like petrol, and paper, which the Sinn Feiners possess. At elections they flood the whole place with leaflets, and they go everywhere in motor cars. How is that paid for? Whence comes the paper? You never hear of appeals for money. There are no popular associations for the people to join with annual, or monthly, subscriptions for the benefit of the Cause. Sinn Fein organizes meetings, and produces speakers ad lib, it runs shops which obviously cannot be self supporting, and it comes amongst a population which is perfectly indifferent, and gradually leads it astray, but it never asks for a penny. When there are meetings in public halls a small price is asked for admittance, 3d or for some seats 6d. Not to charge as much as that would look odd, but to charge so little does not pay the whole expense of the meeting I should think, at the present price of gas.

Then there is queer talk getting up amongst the people which can only come from Germany. Tilly, who is a Protestant, slowly dying in the workhouse, told X [unidentified] that 'the Kaiser loves Ireland'. It gave both X and me an awful turn. And there was that silly youth who said that in nine months England would be beaten and Ireland and Germany would be friends.

RS to KS 24 April 1918

[*Belfast disturbances, c. 280 words.*] Ireland has now been under mob law for very nearly six years. I count that mob law began on June 29 1912. That was when the Hibernians attacked the Sunday School, and a week later came the ship yard outrages.[73] The Hibernians were run in, and sent to jail, but a whole number of ship yard outrages were never punished, and it was that summer that Sir Edward Carson saw the Kaiser, and that autumn that the Covenant was signed. But the mob cannot rule forever. It gets worn out with its own vagaries at last. Then comes despotism, and if we get a good despot we might yet do very well. The mob will have learnt a certain amount of wisdom from its misfortunes, and someday Ireland will put its considerable energies into something sensible.

RS to KS, 25 April 1918

You remember that Sinn Fein shop that I found locked?[74] Well I went there again to get a badge that X wanted. It was again locked, and again the girl opened it, her mother came to serve and convinced me finally that she is a paid agent of Germany. I said 'You keep late hours on the Falls Road.' She said 'Yes we are a tobacco shop and our chief business is in the evening.' I looked at every little shop along the road as I went away, and they all had their doors open. I began to read a notice put up at the back of the shop. It said the shop never stocked English goods if they could possibly get others. It stocked Irish goods, or goods from countries 'friendly to Ireland'. The woman offered to move some boxes which stood in front of the notice. I said 'oh no matter. I see what it is about.' She said something about not stocking English tobacco, I said 'Is tobacco grown in England?' She said it was manufactured in England. Now and then they stocked Dutch tobacco.

'It is just what is manufactured in *England* we do not stock.' A woman who had come in began to snigger. I observe that when I get that shop open someone always does come in, queer people generally, but always someone. 'We have a prejudice against England' said the shop-woman in a most provocative tone 'You could not expect anything else.' 'Oh' said I 'You need not tell me that. I have lived in Ireland all my life, and I know what Sinn Fein is made of' and I walked out before she could answer. I had meant to say 'I know Sinn Fein is made in Germany' but I changed it. Could anything be less like a real shopwoman?

She is not nearly as good as the old man in the central place. He is really an engaging old man. Your heart goes out to him as he brings out his sedition. He is so very anxious to please you, and to get exactly the sedition you will like, and he falls in with your humour at once. This woman drags politics in by the head and the heels, and is so sneering and aggressive, she would put you against any side. She has very much the tone you expect in an Ulster Volunteer, what their admirers call 'grim' 'the sterling gruffness of the hardy northern character.' It fits in very badly with secrecy and plotting. I would give something to see the German records in which people like that appear. *[Notes on cottage visits and the role of clergy in the UVF, c. 500 words.]*

[Break in letter sequence, from 25 April 1918 to 2 September 1918]

November 1918

[First page missing.] . . . accept it. I sat down at the table and began some Guild business. Suddenly I heard clank clank clank. And it was St Mary's solitary bell. Not ringing as for service, but going anyhow as if a child were pulling the rope. And I took up my hat again and ran into the street and X after me and all the people were at their doors along the street, and X stood at the door here, and I ran into Crumlin Road and there was a little group of men, and I said 'What is it?' and they said 'It's the peace' and the Crumlin Road was full of people running towards the Church. But there was no one there and after a

minute the bell left off clanking, and I talked with the two men for a
second or two, and they said 'It is unconditional surrender' and I went
back and X was at the door and her special crony Mrs. McClaren from
next door was with her, and I told them I would run down to Bairds
and get a paper for I knew there would be a special edition.[75] The
morning papers did not bring out special editions oddly enough. On
such a day I would have waited if there was not enough paper to bring
out two editions. I ran as hard as I could with decency to Agnes Street
and we had to wait a good two minutes for the tram and it seemed like
half an hour. And down we went to Bairds, and it was there the press
was, and boys selling the papers in the streets. I got out a penny and
gave it to the boy and while I was giving it would you believe he was
asking two pence and a man beside me was saying 'Oh the price of the
Telegraph was only a penny' But said the boy Germany has surrendered. So I gave him twopence and said I was glad to pay for such
news. And I just glanced at the paper and saw it was unconditional surrender. And I folded it up and put it in my pocket and sped up again
to go to Mrs. Halfpenny. On the way I ran in to X and gave her the
heading to look at. No one wanted more than that. You may fancy
what our reduced tram service is like when I tell you I footed it all the
way from Baird's to Agnes Street before the tram overtook me. So
then up I went to Mrs. Halfpenny's. The Crumlin road was very full.
All the schools are closed for the flu, so the children were all over
everywhere.[76] When I got to her house she was there with one of her
daughters, in floods of tears. 'Now mother here is Miss Stephen. Now
is it true?' 'Yes it is quite true. I have brought the paper.' But Mrs.
Halfpenny would only go on 'And where is my Jim?' So I took the
paper and began to read some absurd stuff I do not know what about
the Kaiser flying in a tourist's cap and enjoying a cigarette unmoved
somewhere or other, and that interested her, and gradually she calmed
down and said 'And little Malachi will soon be home'. We then began
to speculate how he and Pat had felt when they heard 'the cease fire'.
It was sounded I believe by French time, but with us it was only about
half past eleven then for I really had run like a hare. So then I went on

to old Mrs. Whelan and she said Oh when were the prisoners coming home and it was very grim because I know she expects her Tim to be with them in spite of the war office saying that he is dead. And then I went to Mrs. Rice and she sat by the fire saying 'I am very glad. I am very glad' and really she did not care two straws because her Ownie was killed in action and Jo is in a lunatic asylum with shell shock. She is very fond of those two boys. I could hardly bear either of them, they were the sort you never saw sober. Then I went to Mrs. McCorry and that was the first really cheerful house. She is sure her Hugh will be home by Christmas and she will send him down to see me. He is an interned sea man and was torpedoed while going to fetch us some meat from South America. And I sent him some books while he was in prison. I then proceeded to Mrs. Delany. She said was it true? I said yes and began to read the paper. She explained that she had been in bed with the flu, and the baker came and said the war was over, and she got straight out of bed and came to sit by the fire and see what she would hear, she could not lie in bed when the war was over, and God had blessed 'this family'. Neither her own brothers nor her husband's brothers have been killed, though badly wounded some of them, but no one is dead 'even to distant friends'. Alas it was her husband wanted to go and she would not let him, because the widows get such a small pension. However all his brothers went and hers too. From that I called in to Dan McAvey's the Sinn Feiners. He lives exactly opposite Halfpenny's and the girls go in and help him keep the shop. Sarah Jane Halfpenny was there yesterday. I said I wanted back a book I had left for him, and Sarah Jane said he had gone down the town 'to see the fun'. So he walked up the street and I said he was to let me have Bryce's Holy Roman Empire back and would he like another and he said Yes something similar. Mrs. Halfpenny said in a whisper that it was a sad day for him but he looks to be standing it well. So I made no unpleasant remarks. After lunch I went to Mrs. Murray if that is her name. She lives in Flax Street and her son was wounded in seven places after the retreat from Mons and has been P[risoner] of W[ar] ever since. She told me she had heard nothing till eleven o'clock and then she heard the horns and could not think what it was, and then the girls ran in from their work and said 'Mother the war is over the manager has announced it' and I said 'Why is it not pleasanter?' and she said 'Well I know if my son comes and stands in that door way it will kill me' and I said 'But he will write first' and she said 'Yes write or telegraph, but I feel as if it were going to kill me.' However the prospect of being killed was evidently not too disagreeable under the circumstances. Then I went to Mrs. Donaldson and she said 'It is sad. It is sad' and Mary Catherine a brisk young thing of 40 or so said the news is very good. So I said to Mrs. Donaldson 'Are you thinking of your grandson?' and she said 'Yes and more than I did the day he was killed' and the strange part of it is that it is the dead grandson she thinks of not the other who is P of W. Then I went to Mrs. Quigly, and she had the flu and was nursing three children with flu, and she did not care a hang. 'Oh their father will look after them when he comes back. He is very good with them, and we shall have coals now and flour, and all we want.' And then I had one quite horrid visit to Mrs. McArdle the mother of that Pat or whatever he calls himself who came to tea with you. She is I am sure nearly sixty, and so very superior, and she was that drunk she could hardly get across the room. She kept partly laughing about it and partly apologising, and she was rather frightened too. But it was horrid. She said she had taken a glass because the war was over. I was just as glad all the Owens were out for I had expected the same with them but not at Mrs. McArdle's and her old brother in law was sober for once, but said his wife had also been drinking. It was really very horrid. Happily I did not see her. So then it was getting dark and I wondered if it was a little hard on them to visit too late on such a very wonderful day and I went home. Then it seemed that X wanted to go and see what was going on in town. So we went out at about 7.30. It was the weirdest sight and as far as I can understand Dublin was the very same. The streets were very nearly dark. Only about one lamp in three lit and that burning very dim. And the bigger streets were crowded. It was not quite like an ordinary Belfast crowd because there was no centre of attraction. The people were just streaming about everywhere. And you got to places where you walk easily, and you got where you were so pushed that we had to hold tight together not to get lost. There were soldiers and sailors lots of them, and some were sober and some a good bit the reverse, and quite a number were dancing in the middle of the road, and all nearly dark. There were Orange bands, and Salvation Army bands, and all sorts of bands and they ran here and there discoursing any music they knew, and each had a crowd running with it, and they surged past in the dim light. It was very foggy too and the trams were running to a small extent. We saw a notice that there would be a short service at the Cathedral at eight so we went in about 8.10 to see what was going on.[77] I wondered as we went up to the door would it be full or would it be a desert with a dozen of a congregation I was quite prepared for either. But it was full cram jam full as packed as it would hold. The Dean was preaching, I am sure I do not know what he was saying, but nothing party I did notice that. Then came the Lord's Prayer and the Old Hundredth very fine from such a crowd, and then or before an extempore prayer. What that said I am not at all sure, but the brightly lit Church and the great silent crowd were very striking after the dark queer streets. When it ended we went to the streets again and we fell in with Miss Bushe and Millicent Rush and we all rambled about together holding hands and at last there came some little interruption and Miss Bushe let go my hand and was lost to sight in a second. But I kept a good grip on X as she is too blind and rather too imaginative to be left alone in such a scene. I should not like her to be there without me or some trustworthy guide. She is also full of adventure. The worst was her having to stand all the time in the Cathedral it was impossible to get a seat. I was very tired getting in, and woke too early this morning. This was only to be expected.

After breakfast I went again to the cottages. I mean to try and see them all but I did not get through many. I am more than a little tired and cannot sleep it off as I should if I were less tired. Some of them gave me quite a pretty account of the announcement at the mills yesterday. First they heard the machinery leave off, and they wondered what it was, then the manager came and said the war was over. I asked what the manager had said and the woman telling me said 'He did not very well know himself what he was saying but he told them.' And some of the women nearly fainted, I could fancy that. One child waved a handkerchief (I suppose it was a child's trick it may have been a woman's) but anyway this handkerchief was waved and it was white and a voice shouted 'Germany's flag' and then they all sang all the war songs they knew, and they were quite mad, and the foreman sent them home because of course no one was going to work any more. But it was all the height of good temper. Today the hooters went as usual at half past six but so few appeared that the works were closed at breakfast time. I think they will work again tomorrow and I hope they will for the men workers are getting mischievous. They really are a bore. They came up in the crowd and emptied a bread cart. You know the great high things, they got all the loaves out at the back while the man was driving very slowly not to crush anyone. Our baker kept all in the back streets, to avoid a similar fate. Also we hear of shops being pilfered, and people stopped in the roads and made to dance like Mafeking night you know.[78] Dublin seems just the same but I hear of nothing angry and am much relieved because I felt by no means sure.

So who did I see this morning. Mrs. Lenehan. She and her sister Cassy McNulty were together. They both looked perfectly radiant. It is really very nice for her. Her husband was not really obliged to go. He was through the South African war and is pretty old, and he joined all over again and had to learn quite a new method of warfare, and he has been through the whole from the beginning I think without a scratch. She says 'It is peace, and we have won' with a triumph that I have not met so far. The worst is she says she and Cassie had half a pint yesterday to 'make them happy'. Dear me. Was the news not enough to make them happy without the half pint? She says they cannot have any more today because they cannot afford it. But she is in a sort of triumphant state of mind that rather pleases me. McAlise mother and daughter are rather taken up with the flu which the old mother appears to have and will not tend.

At no. 10 I annexed a new friend that I had been hearing about, Mrs. Connor to wit. She looks quite young but has been nine years married, and her husband was killed in action on Sep 4th. She says it would be less bad if he had been killed early in the war, but that this does seem like the last minute, and she finds the rejoicings very trying. From that I went to Cassidy's. Sarah Nelson that was Sarah Cassidy has also lost her husband at the last minute a month later than Connor. Also John Henry Cassidy has had his leg blown off which I think I told you before. And the last house was Kitty Madden's where they are so anxious about Willy Reed that they are lighting no candles. He has dysentery or some such in Egypt on his way home from Mese. I am to write to the Red Cross.

I meant to have gone out to some more but when I came in I felt I really could not go out again. There is no use in making quite too great a push though there are lots more that I want to see. Oh one person I must tell about and that is Mrs. Smyth. I met her in the road this morning and took her in to call on X. She does come to call now and again as she lives quite alone. She was bubbling over like Mrs. Lenehan 'Yes Yes We have the peace. I shall get my boy home again. Willy will come from Malta. I had some wee girls in with me last night. A party of them. Well we had the door shut. No one knew but we sang all the songs we knew and then we were dancing. I danced all round the kitchen and my shoes are so old they fell off, and the wee girls put them on again (She is very rheumatic and stoops with great difficulty). I was in town and I never thought and all at once came the news, and I caught hold of a lamp post lest I would fall, and I called out "Glory be to God it's over" and a man came up and gave me a wee Union Jack, and I ran away home and I was dancing in the street and waving my flag and the neighbours ran out and said Mrs. Smyth is it true? And I said Yes Yes It's true and they all ran away down and got Union Jacks and we have them in Oakfield Street (this is true it is the only Roman street to show flags) and mine is hanging over the mantelpiece I shall keep it all my life and have it buried in my coffin. And this morning one of the wee girls wrote a letter for me to Willy and I posted it, and it says "Come home soon and call in by the way and see Kaiser Bill"'. So X had five o'clock tea about twelve in the morning and this gay old soul partook with a very good will. She really is a nice old thing, and her Willy enlisted quite at the first.

Now I think I shall post this. It is a peace letter.

Abbreviations

DJS	Dorothea Jane Stephen
DUGS	Dublin University Gaelic Society
IV	Irish Volunteers
KS	Katharine Stephen
RCB	Representative Church Body
RIC	Royal Irish Constabulary
RS	Rosamond Stephen
TCD	Trinity College, Dublin
UVF	Ulster Volunteer Force

Notes to Introduction

1 RS to DJS, 28 June 1910.
2 MS. 253, 'The Record' 1902–1940, Representative Church Body Library, Dublin.
3 Sir James Fitzjames Stephen (1829–1894). Second son of Sir James Stephen and Jane Venn, called to the bar in 1854; Secretary to the Education Commission in 1858. Wrote regularly for the *Saturday Review*, *Cornhill Magazine,* and the *Pall Mall Gazette*.
4 Sir James Stephen (1789–1859). Called to the bar, 1811; Colonial Under-Secretary from 1836 to 1847; appointed Regius Professor of Modern History at Cambridge in 1849. Also held a Professorship at the East India College, Haileybury, and wrote for journals including the *Edinburgh Review*.
5 Katharine Stephen (1856–1924). Vice-Principal of Newnham College, 1892–1911, Principal, 1911–1920. Author of a *French History for English Children* and *Three Sixteenth-Century Sketches*.
6 Revd. J.W. Cunningham.
7 Revd. John Venn.
8 William Conyngham Plunket (1828–1897). Educated TCD, active against disestablishment, but prominent in the reorganisation of the church after 1870. Archbishop of Dublin, 1884 and Dean of Christ Church Cathedral, 1884–7.
9 RS to KS, 9 Apr. 1917.
10 Stephen always differentiated between Catholics, meaning members of the Anglican Church, and Roman Catholics.
11 Introduction to 'The Record'.

12   Alan Acheson estimates that the Church of Ireland spent over eight million
      pounds on philanthropic and administrative expenses between 1871 and 1915. *A*
      History of the Church of Ireland 1691–1996 (Dublin, 1997), pp. 205–6.

13   It was not until 1920 that women were again permitted to serve on Select
      Vestries.

14   RS to DJS, 3 Oct. 1911, 'The Record'.

15   Stephen travelled constantly between Belfast and Huntingdon in England, where
      her mother still lived, between 1902 and 1912. On her mother's death, she
      moved permanently to Ireland, living in Belfast until 1919, then in Dublin until
      1931, when she moved to County Louth. A short time before her death in 1951
      she moved back to England to live with her sister, Katharine.

16   RS to DJS, 3 Oct. 1911.

17   Note appended to 'The Record' by Stephen in January 1940.

18   RS to KS, 25 Apr. 1918.

19   RS to DJS, 10 Jan. 1916.

20   RS to DJS, 3 Oct. 1911, 'The Record'.

21   RS to DJS, 3 Aug. 1915.

22   RS to DJS, 5 May 1916.

23   RS to DJS, 22 Apr. 1918.

24   Catholic enlistment was, as Stephen states in her letters, high in Belfast, and pro-
      portionately exceeded that of Protestants in certain counties in 1915. David Fitz-
      patrick, 'The Logic of Collective Sacrifice: Ireland and the British Army,
      1914–1918', *The Historical Journal*, 38, 4 (1995), pp. 1024–5.

25   John and his brother William had great faith in the potential for unity which mil-
      itary service held. *Terence Denman, A Lonely Grave: the life and death of William Red-*
      mond (Dublin, 1995), p. 103.

26   This strategy was successful up to a point: The Home Rule Act was passed in Sep-
      tember, but was suspended for the duration of the war, which all believed would
      be a matter of months. Redmond's decisive action appears to have been initially
      broadly supported, but the continuation of the war, and the rising nationalist
      movement in Ireland, combined to turn public opinion against him.

27   Fitzpatrick, 'Collective Sacrifice', p. 1018.

28   RS to KS, 23 Nov. 1914.

29   RS to DJS, 21 Aug. 1917.

30   Fearing violent opposition to conscription in Ireland, the government avoided its
      imposition. When it finally decided to conscript Irishmen in April 1918, Henry
      Duke, the chief secretary for Ireland, pinpointed the problem: 'We might almost
      as well conscript Germans'. Quoted in James Lydon, *The Making of Ireland: From*
      Ancient Times to the Present (London, 1998), p. 344.

31   RS to KS, 17 Mar. 1916.

32   RS to DJS, 13 May 1916.

33   RS to DJS, 28 July 1915.

34   RS to DJS, 27 Feb. 1917.

35   RS to DJS, 19 June 1917.

36   Quoted in an obituary in the *Church of Ireland Gazette*, 2 Mar. 1951.

Notes to Narrative

1   Sir Edward Henry Carson (1854–1935). Lawyer, MP, and leader of the Irish Unionist Party. Attorney General (1915); First Lord of the Admiralty (1917), and member of the War Cabinet without Portfolio, 1917–18.

2   John Edward Redmond (1851–1918). Lawyer, MP, and leader of the Irish Parliamentary Party (1900).

3   A meeting had been held on 15 November, to protest against the dismissal from the Ordnance Department of Robert Monteith, 'a Captain in the Sinn Fein section of the Irish Volunteers' (*Irish Times*, 16 Nov. 1914). It was addressed by the O'Rahilly, Constance Markievicz and James Connolly, all of whom urged Irishmen to join the Irish Citizen Army or the Volunteers, and called for German success in the war.

4   John Pentland Mahaffy, Vice-Provost of Trinity College, objected to an invitation from the Dublin University Gaelic Society to Patrick Pearse to address the Society, and had the meeting banned. Mahaffy's correspondence with the DUGS was published in the *Irish Times* on 14 Nov. 1914.

5   Founded by Arthur Griffith in 1905, Sinn Féin ('Ourselves') rose to prominence after the 1916 Rising, with which it was incorrectly credited.

6   Honorary Secretary to the Ladies' Recruiting Committee in Dublin.

7   A recruiting march had taken place in Belfast, which culminated with speeches to a large crowd outside City Hall. *Irish Times*, 20 Nov. 1914.

8   The 6th Connaught Rangers and the 6th Royal Irish Regiment, both part of the 47th Brigade, were based in a military training camp near Fermoy, County Cork.

9   Emily lived at Tinakilly House, Avoca, County Wicklow. See MS 10247/12/49 for the 1916 diary of her sister, Winifred, or MS 10247/12/35 for the 1917 diary of Alice Katherine Wynne, her mother, both in TCD.

10 There was an increase in emigration to avoid conscription throughout the country. In Connaught, police estimated that by June 1914 1,344 men had emigrated to escape the threat. In Roscommon alone, '200 farmers' sons had fled to the United States' to avoid being conscripted. Thomas Hennessey, *Dividing Ireland: World War I and Partition* (London, 1998), p. 101.

11   Established in 1890 in order to deal with the economic problems of the West of Ireland.

12   A fishing community in Galway.

13   In a 1947 note appended to this letter, Stephen wrote: 'Mrs. Carr was a London dressmaker who made me a purple satin dress in the style then known as "Princess". It was specially designed to stand packing in [a] small space, and I wore it on a visit of two or three days, in the Palace at Tuam. It was my only evening dress.'

14   Stephen Lucius Gwynn (1864–1950). MP (for Galway City, 1906–18, not East Galway), author and journalist, and member of the Irish Convention 1917–18.

15   At Finner, near Ballyshannon.

16   The Mater Infirmorum Hospital, Crumlin Road.

17   The Royal Victoria Hospital, Grosvenor Road.

18   Military training camp, in County Kildare.

19   John and Ishbel Gordon, Lord and Lady Aberdeen. On leaving Ireland at the end of his second term as Lord Lieutenant (1886, and 1905–15), the Earl of Aberdeen was promoted to 'Marquess of Aberdeen and Temair', 'the addition evoking Ireland without any attachment to an estate'. Doris French, *Ishbel and the Empire: A Biography of Lady Aberdeen* (Toronto, 1988), p. 294.

20   The Belgian Band was 'composed of leading musicians from the King of the Belgian's Orchestra, the Royal Opera, Brussels, and other Belgian orchestras. The band is composed of genuine refugees, and its members are either wounded soldiers or men too old for active service. There are twenty-two members in the band, every one of whom is a talented musician.' *Irish Times*, 1 June 1915.

21   Of this performance, the *Northern Whig* commented: 'In addition to the star item, there are several other enjoyable turns on the programme . . . The moving picture this week is in bad taste, and should be left out of the programme.' 8 June 1915.

22   Rheims Cathedral was shelled by German forces on 20 September 1914.

23   There were military training camps at Ballykinler and Clandeboye, County Down.

24   On 29 June 1915, the National Registration Bill was introduced by Walter Long, Colonial Secretary, 'to put the potential services of every citizen at the State's disposal in this hour of extreme danger.' Every household was to register males and females between the ages of 15 and 65, although registration was voluntary in Ireland's case. W.J. Reader, *At Duty's Call: A Study in Obsolete Patriotism* (Manchester, 1988), p. 125.

25   Queen's Island, Belfast, where the city's shipyards were located. In July 1912 Catholic workers were attacked and expelled, following a clash between Home Rulers and Orangemen at Castledawson, County Londonderry on July 2. Jonathan Bardon, *A History of Ulster* (Belfast, 1992), p. 436.

26 The meeting was actually held in City Hall, and was addressed by Alderman Lawrence O'Neill. 'Several speakers strongly urged resistence to conscription in the event of the Government attempting to enforce it in Ireland.' *Irish Times* 21 July 1915.

27 The *Lusitania* was torpedoed by Germany off the southern coast of Ireland on 7 May 1915, with the loss of 1,198 lives.

28 'Yous' is the Dublin form of 'you'.

29 Jeremiah O'Donovan Rossa (1831–1915). Fenian, Irish Republican Brotherhood member, imprisoned in 1859 and 1865. Exiled to America in 1871, he died in New York. Buried in Glasnevin cemetery, Dublin. Patrick Pearse rallied supporters with his funeral oration: '. . . the fools, the fools, the fools! — they have left us our Fenian dead, and while Ireland holds these graves, Ireland unfree will never be at peace.'

30 Sir Roger Casement (1864–1916). Diplomat and nationalist. Attempted to raise an Irish Brigade from prisoners of war in Berlin in 1914. Returned to Ireland in 1916 to postpone the Rising; captured, tried and sentenced to death. Hanged 3 August 1916.

31 Sir Horace Curzon Plunkett (1854–1932). Founder and President of the Irish Agricultural Organization Society. Head of the Irish Convention of 1917–18; Senator (1922), left Ireland following the burning of his home by Republicans in 1923.

32 John Dillon (1851–1927). Anti-Parnellite Irish Parliamentary Party member, MP (Mayo East 1885–1918). Leader of the IPP (1918); led party out of the House of Commons on the introduction of the Military Service Bill (April 1918).

33 Joseph Devlin (1872–1934). Irish Parliamentary Party member, MP (North Kilkenny 1902-6; West Belfast 1906–18, and Falls Division Belfast 1918–22).

34 A cleaner who worked at the Settlement.

35 A prisoner of war whose family Stephen visited in Belfast.

36 A charitable organisation established to send parcels to prisoners of war.

37 The *Northern Whig* and the *Belfast News Letter*, both Unionist newspapers.

38 Although RS in 'The Record' states that 'Aasleagh' is in County Galway, she appears to be referring to Athleague, just over the county border in County Roscommon.

39 Another settlement worker.

40 Same letter.

41 Guild of Witness. Established by RS in 1901 as part of the Church of Ireland Union of Prayer, it worked to strengthen the presence of the church in Ireland, especially in rural areas. See 'The Record', introduction.

42 RS had heard a rumour (actually untrue) that eight men had been taken from Dublin to Belfast and shot in Victoria Barracks there.

43 Patrick Henry Pearse (1879–1916). Dublin-born lawyer, founder member of the Irish Volunteers, and member of the Irish Republican Brotherhood, he founded St. Enda's school in 1908. Declared the Irish Republic from the steps of the General Post Office. Surrendered 19 April, executed 3 May.

44 Thomas MacDonagh (1878–1916). Academic and playwright, co-founder of St. Edna's and the Irish Volunteers, member of the IRB. Signatory to the 1916 Proclamation, executed 3 May 1916.

45 Thomas James Clarke (1857–1916). Convicted of dynamiting offences in England, 1883. Sentenced to life imprisonment, released 1898, emigrated to America. Returned to Ireland 1907. First signatory to the 1916 Proclamation. Served in the GPO in the Rising, executed 3 May 1916.

46 It was indeed the same person. Imprisoned following the Rising, he attended the AGM of the Irish Guild of the Church on his release, and moved to rescind a resolution passed in June 1916 condemning the rising. Irvine claimed that 'the Church is doing its best to drive everybody like that [meaning himself, a Protestant nationalist] out, and to hound them down.' *Church of Ireland Gazette,* 17 May 1918.

47 The offices of the *Irish Times* are located in Westmoreland Street.

48 Constance Markievicz (née Gore-Booth 1868–1927). Born in Sligo, married Count Casimir Markievicz in 1900. Despite her Ascendancy background, she became increasingly involved in radical socialism and nationalism. President of Cumann na mBan, she opposed the Treaty in 1922.

49 Maud Gonne MacBride (1866–1953). Born in Aldershot, active in radical Irish and French politics in the 1880s and 1890s. Co-founded Inghinidhe na hÉireann in 1900, married Major John MacBride in 1903, formally separated in 1905. Remained a political radical, although less supportive of violence, after First World War.

50 Joseph Mary Plunkett (1887–1916). Son of George Noble Plunkett, a Papal Count. Poet, and editor of the *Irish Review,* 1913–14. Active in the Irish Volunteers, despite poor health, and a member of the Irish Republican Brotherhood. Sentenced to death for his part in the Rising, married Grace Gifford on the eve of his execution in Kilmainham Jail.

51 T.C. Butterfield. He wrote to RS in April 1916, suggesting that she write some articles detailing the benefits to Ireland in concluding the war swiftly, so as to reduce her share of the debt.

52 Sir Roger Casement.

53 Three people were killed and thirty-eight injured on 26 July 1914 at Bachelor's Walk, Dublin by the King's Own Scottish Borderers, who were being taunted by a crowd following the successful landing of arms for the Volunteers at Howth.

54 Henry Edward Duke (1855–1939). Judge and politician. Called to the bar in 1885, became Chief Secretary for Ireland (1916–18) after the 1916 Rising.

55 The Irish Convention opened in July 1917, chaired by Horace Plunkett. It was intended as an opportunity for differing political groups in Ireland to resolve the situation, but only the Redmondites and the southern unionists fully supported it. Sinn Fein refused to attend, the Ulster unionists refused to consider any compromise, and the initiative therefore ended in failure.

56 Carson was First Lord of the Admiralty from December 1916 until his resignation in July 1917.

57 The Protection of Person and Property Act was passed in March 1881, and allowed for the detention without trial of persons 'reasonably suspected of treasonable activity'.

58 Arthur MacMurrough Kavanagh (1831–1889). Born without proper limbs. Justice of the Peace, MP for County Wexford 1866-8, and County Carlow, 1868–80. A conservative in politics, he actually lost his seat in 1880, not 1885.

59 One of the Catholic shipbuilders driven out in 1912.

60 Sir Bryan Mahon (1862–1930). A Boer War veteran, he led the celebrated relief of Mafeking on 17 May 1900. Commander of Salonika Army, 1915–16, and Commander-in-Chief in Ireland, 1916–18.

61 William Tarrant Browne (1865–1939). Educated TCD, Curate of St. Mary's, Belfast, 1896–98; Rector of Killyleagh, 1908–29.

62 William Hoey Kearney Redmond (1861–1917). Politician and soldier. MP for Wexford Borough, North Fermanagh, Cork City and East Clare, he persuaded the war office to commission him in February 1915, despite his age. He was killed in action with the 6th Royal Irish at Messines.

63 Redmond was 56 years of age, and had been refused permission to join his battalion, the 6th Royal Irish Regiment, in an attack upon Wytschaete village, Ypres. He finally threatened to disobey orders or resign his commission, so that Lieutenant Colonel Edmund Roche-Kelly, his battalion CO, eventually agreed to let him go. He was wounded in the leg and wrist, and died at 6.30 pm on 7 June 1917. John Redmond, the Chaplain to the Ulster Division, helped to dress his wounds, and sent William's last message to his wife. Denman, *A Lonely Grave: The Life and Death of William Redmond* pp. 119–20.

64 Thomas Ashe (1885–1917). Leader of the County Meath Volunteers during the 1916 Rising, Ashe was imprisoned for making seditious speeches in August 1917. He led a hunger strike for political status, and died while being force-fed.

65 The Defence of the Realm Act.

66 Ivor Churchill Guest, Lord Wimborne (1873–1939). Liberal MP 1906–14; Postmaster General, 1910–12, Lord Lieutenant of Ireland, 1915–16 and 1916–18.

67 Alice Milligan (1866–1953). Methodist poet and playwright, founding co-editor of *Shan Van Vocht*, and active in the Gaelic League.

68 On 28 February Clare was declared a Special Military Area to allow for the suppression of agrarian disorder. Restrictions on meetings and personal movement were soon after imposed. David Fitzpatrick, *Politics and Irish Life, 1913–21: Provincial Experience of War and Revolution* (Dublin, 1977), p. 151.

69 Sinn Féin had been conducting an anti-conscription campaign for some time, but it was not until 21 April that a nationwide signing of the anti-conscription pledge, which stated that signatories would 'solemnly . . . resist conscription by the most effective means at our disposal', occurred. Quoted in Hennessey, *Dividing Ireland*, p. 221.

70 Sir Herbert Stephen (1857–1932). Lawyer, clerk of Assize for the Northern Circuit, and Rosamond Stephen's brother.

71 A.M. Sullivan, *The Story of Ireland* (Dublin, 1867; many subsequent editions). It was dedicated to 'My Young Fellow-Countrymen . . . soon to be the Men of Ireland.' W.E.H. Lecky's *History of Ireland in the Eighteenth Century* was published in 1892. An MP for Dublin University, he opposed Home Rule.

72 Lloyd George introduced the Military Service Bill on 10 April, which did not impose conscription on Ireland, but allowed for its imposition by Order in Council when the necessity should arise.

73 See note 25, above.

74 This was a second shop, on the Falls Road, which RS visited on 11 April. She was suspicious that the shop was a front for German conspiracies. Letter to KS, 11 Apr. 1918, 'The Record'.

75 W. & G. Baird, printers of the *Belfast Telegraph*, 124-32 Royal Avenue.

76 'In 1918–19 an influenza pandemic of unprecedented virulence swept the world, killing between 25 and 50 million people.' Deaths in this outbreak therefore killed more than died in the First World War. Roy Porter (ed.), *The Cambridge Illustrated History of Medicine* (Cambridge, 1996), pp. 49–50.

77 St. Anne's Anglican Cathedral, Donegall St.

78 The town of Mafeking, under siege by the Boers for 217 days during the Boer War, was relieved on 17 May 1900 by two British relief columns. The news was rapturously greeted in Britain, where it was heralded as a turning point in the war.

Bibliography

Boyce, D. George, *Ireland 1828–1923: From Ascendancy to Democracy* (Oxford, 1992)
——*The Revolution in Ireland 1879–1923* (London, 1988)

Buckland, Patrick, *Irish Unionism 1: The Anglo-Irish and the New Ireland 1885–1922* (Dublin, 1972)
——*Irish Unionism 2: Ulster Unionism and the Origins of Northern Ireland 1886–1922* (Dublin, 1973)

Denman, Terence, *A Lonely Grave: The Life and Death of William Redmond* (Dublin, 1995)

Fitzpatrick, David (ed.), *Ireland and the First World War* (Dublin, 1986)
——'The Logic of Collective Sacrifice: Ireland and the British Army, 1914–1918', *The Historical Journal*, 38, 4 (1995), pp. 1017–1030
——*The Two Irelands, 1912–1939* (Oxford, 1998)

Garvin, Tom, *Nationalist Revolutionaries in Ireland 1858–1928* (Oxford, 1987)

Hennessey, Thomas, *Dividing Ireland: World War I and Partition* (Routledge, 1998)

Martin, F. X. (ed.), *Leaders and Men of the Easter Rising: Dublin 1916* (London, 1967)
——*The Howth Gun-Running and the Kilcoole Gun-Running, 1914: Recollections and Documents* (Dublin, 1964)

McDowell, R. B., *The Irish Convention 1917–18* (London, 1970)

Miller, David, *Queen's Rebels: Ulster Loyalism in Historical Perspective* (Dublin, 1978)

O'Halpin, Eunan, *The Decline of the Union: British Government in Ireland 1892–1920* (Dublin, 1987)

Orr, Philip, *The Road to the Somme: Men of the Ulster Division Tell Their Story* (Belfast, 1987)

Phoenix, Eamon, *Northern Nationalism: Nationalist Politics, Partition and the Catholic Minority in Northern Ireland 1890–1940* (Belfast, 1994)

Stewart, A. T. Q., *The Ulster Crisis: Resistance to Home Rule 1912–14* (London, 1967)

Townshend, Charles, *Political Violence in Ireland: Government and Resistance Since 1848* (Oxford, 1983)

Willis, Geraldine, 'Rosamond Stephen: a constructive visionary', *New Divinity*, vol. 3, no. 2, winter 1972, pp. 160–5

Index